LAC DE COMO
CERNOBBIO

GRAND HOTEL
VILLA d'ESTE

villa
style
d'este

vill

style

d

a

jean govoni salvadore

foreword by joseph heller

'este

First published in the United States of America in 2000 by
Rizzoli International Publications, Inc.

Copyright © 2000 Giovanna (Jean) Govoni Salvadore
Foreword copyright © Joseph Heller

ISBN 0-8478-2262-1
LC 99-75985

Second edition 2009

Printed in Italy by Brunati Arti Grafiche
22020 S. Fermo - Como - Italy
Tel. +39 031.210554 - Fax +39 031.212058
e-mail: info@brunatiartigrafiche.com - www.brunatiartigrafiche.com

Designed by Divine Design Studio, Inc.

JEANNE MARIE LA CAZE DROULERS

Style has nothing to do with how rich you are or even who you are. Style puts quality before quantity.

It is inborn. Either you have it or you don't. Jeanne Marie La Caze Droulers had style.

During the years of her presidency from 1972 to 1987, she graced the hotel with her warm presence.

She set a standard of patrician hospitality for all of us to follow.

ACKNOWLEDGMENTS

To do justice to the acknowledgments would take several pages, and still I would worry about many names that I might have overlooked. So let me begin with an apology, since I am bound to forget to thank the numerous friends, guests, and staff alike who have provided so much of the material that makes up this book.

My eternal gratitude goes to Marta Hallett, publisher, editor, agent, and above all, friend, whose steadfast support never failed me. There are three other friends I am especially grateful to: Steven Kaufmann, Larry Ashmead, and Mary Ellen Barton; without their unfaltering encouragement, I would never have been able to have conceived this book, let alone write it.

My heartfelt thanks go first to Camillo Livi, who became president of Villa d'Este in 1966 after Marc Droulers died; to Willy Dombré, whose family managed the hotel in the late 19th century; to Mario Arrigo, who started in 1947 and served as manager of the hotel from 1965 to 1993; and to Angelo Poletti, his assistant for 45 years. I met the above gentlemen in 1967, a turning point in my life—when I started doing public relations for Villa d'Este.

I am especially grateful to Jeanne Marie La Caze Droulers, widow of Marc Droulers, and to her son, Jean Marc, who became C.E.O. in 1976.

I am also indebted to all the staff: Claudio Ceccherelli, who joined Villa d'Este as general manager in 1997; Annamaria Duvia, who has ably assisted me for the last 32 years; the concierges, beginning with Carlo Magni, who retired in 1978 after 51 years, Romano Scotti and Remo Castelli, who spent an average of 40 years on the job, and the newcomers (!), Giorgio De Angelis, Fabrizio Mainoni, Giuseppe Pesenti, and Luigi Dova, each of whom have been working behind the concierge desk for 20 to 25 years; and Giorgio Chiesa, who took over that charge in 1999; the maitre d's: Germano Prina and Giordano Rizzi; and captains Eugenio Colzani, Nicola Alberti, Franco Massara, and Giuseppe Annoni, who have each been with the hotel for 20 to 30 years. Thanks go to all the barmen: Stefano Preti, Pierino Dell'Avo, Gianni Malinverni, Mario Ortelli, Ilio Chiocci, Piero Malinverni, Enrico Mastaglio, Graziano Bonelli, and Daniele Manzoni. To Luciano Parolari, the executive chef, who joined the company in 1967; to chef Angelo Bosetti and pastry chefs Luigi Rossi and Fabrizio Bertolla; and at the Grill, maitre d' Salvatore Piazza and chef Giorgio Zanetti. I would also like to thank the reception team: Franca Tanzi, Barbara Cerullo, and Giuseppina Selva. Thanks are due to the head gardener, Renato Butti, to Emilio Vantadori, Anna Moiana, Patrizia Penna, and to all those who work behind the scenes at Villa d'Este, of whom there are more than 200.

I must not forget to mention the friends I made upon arriving on the shores of Lake Como 33 years ago: Arturo and Bebe Stucchi, Erminia and Miletto Sancassani, Carla Porta Musa, Athena and Enrico Besana, Vincenzo Miozza, Beppe Modenese, Mario Allamel, Adriano Martini, Aldo Cicoletti, Pietro Baragiola, Ennio and Maria Tessuto, Valeria and Marisa Sacco, and, more recently, Countess Paola Brichetto Arnaboldi. Their reminiscences about Villa d'Este's golden days after World War II were invaluable.

In writing this book, I received assistance from all parts of the world, and I would like to list some names of friends who helped me see Villa d'Este in new ways through their eyes; their stories and anecdotes that I have collected over the years deserve to be published in a separate book one day.

Piva Meyer from London is on the top of this list. We figured out that she has visited Villa d'Este for the last 50 years. Jean and Marshall Tulin have reached the 40-year mark along with Mel Goldfeder, who counts close to 30 consecutive years of visits. The same can be said about Helen Menczel. Kathleen and Fred Krehbiel, Ida and Perry Fishbein, Nina and Jens Werner, Ann and Leland Verner, Francine and Halbert Drexler, Beverly and Bill Ehrman, Molly and James McIlvenny, Barbara and Manfred Stalla, Veronica and Stuart Timperley, Gianna and Serafino Cantatore, Deane and William Conley, Marilyn and Jim Black, Phyllis and Mannie Rappaport, and Karen and Charles Hale have been coming to the hotel with their families year after year.

Anita and Paul De Domenico of Santa Fe have spent 15 consecutive summers at Villa d'Este with their children. Now we are expecting the third generation of De Domenicos.

A few more names of friends who have contributed as goodwill ambassadors for Villa d'Este around the world include Sheila and Marty Schott, Mary and Lewis Schott, Jane Taylor, John Kiley, Gene Silbert, Michael and Judie Lacher, Bill Grose, Mary Homi, Ellen Sweeney, Mary Louise Oates and Bob Schrum, Richard and Alix Barthelmes, Karen Kriendler Nelson, Harriette Delsener, Don and Carol Shaw, Karon Cullen, Lucy and Jim Bonorris, Joe Giacoponello, Anne Goodman, Eve and Bill Lilley, Beth and Skip Keesal, Alice Gesar, Maria Battaglia, Margaret and Murray Hendricks, Shelagh Daniels and Albert Shapir, Edith and Hector Siracusano, Walter Matthews, Edward De Luca, Eleonora and Ernst Brunner, Amanda and Lawrence Finn, Franco Bertolasi, and Shelley and David Stevens.

Beginning in the 1970s, Mary and Theo Rossi made annual trips from Australia to Villa d'Este with their ten children to celebrate birthdays, honeymoons, and anniversaries. In later years, when the children grew up, they arrived with their spouses; there are now more than 30 grandchildren waiting for their turn to visit.

The Rossis may have put Villa d'Este on the map in Australia, but there are other faithful friends who consider the hotel their "home away from home." Ian and Judith Forbes have stayed with us for six weeks at a time for each of the last 25 years. Included in the Australian contingent—filling the hotel when winter sets down under—are Christine Hogan, Barbara and Bernie Leser, Elizabeth Rich, Bruce Jarrett, John and Jerry Henderson, Eve Harman, Beverley Sutherland Smith, Leo Schofield, Bill Peach, Caroline Lockhart, Marion von Alderstein, Sharon Storrier-Lyneham, my godchildren Danielle Rossi Helms and Samantha Slaney, Hanna Pan, Julie Keegan, and New Zealander Sir Ron Brierley.

I am eternally indebted to our friends the travel agents.

The media have provided invaluable documentation in their many stories and articles: Stan and Laddie Delaplane, Herb Caen, Pamela Fiori, Geri Trotta, Anita Draycott, Steven and Alexandra Mayes Birnbaum, Leonard and Sylvia Lyons, Jane Montant, Fleur Champin, Geraldine Fabrikant, Nancy Novogrod, Clive Irving, Fred and Eileen Ferretti, David Leavitt and Mark Mitchell, Army and Selma Archerd, Bill Wright, and many others.

Photographers who have taught me to view the beauty of the lake through their lenses include Ronny Jacques, Slim Aarons, Helmut Newton, Victor Skrebneski, Chris Sanders, Brooks Walker, and Fernando Bengoechea.

Thank you, thank you!

Finally, I'd like to give credit to my family, who certainly enjoy their brief visits to Villa d'Este. However, the one who best appreciates the lifestyle of the hotel is my grandson, young Luca Salvadore Tolan.

contents

VILLA D'ESTE VISITORS CIRCA 1910
IN FRONT OF THE FAMED MOSAIC.

foreword

I had not expected ever to write the introductory text for a book devoted to the history and elegance of a luxurious resort hotel, as this book is about the Villa d'Este, outside the Italian village of Cernobbio on Lake Como. But my friendship with Jean Salvadore is strong, my relationship with the management cordial, and the accommodations always thoroughly fulfilling, and it seemed an easier choice, when invited, to comply than to cope with guilty feelings of regret at the appearance of a lack of gratitude and a lack of affection for the people and the place toward which I feel so much. And the book, as you can see by opening it now to just about any page, like the splendid establishment it describes, is easy to praise.

OPPOSITE: THE ORIGINAL ARCHWAY CREATED BY CAROLINE OF BRUNSWICK, FUTURE QUEEN OF ENGLAND, IN 1815, WHEN SHE PURCHASED THE VILLA (PREVIOUSLY KNOWN AS VILLA GARROVO) FROM THE COUNTESS VITTORIA PINO. ABOVE: THE ENTRANCE OF VILLA D'ESTE AS IT APPEARS TODAY.

My acquaintance with Jean Salvadore goes back now almost ten years. A widow of Italian descent, she is a woman of a kind one occasionally meets, usually European, with an adventurous past whose effect upon others she with modesty underestimates.

Though we have know each other for less than a decade, it is highly possible that our paths crossed in Rome more than once over 50 years ago, when I, as a 21-year-old boy in the American Air Corps, came there several times on recreation leave, and she, as a young teenage girl born in Paris of Italian parents and living in Rome, secured employment serving coffee and doughnuts to Americans at the large Red Cross facility in efficient operation there soon after the Germans withdrew from the open city and the advancing Allied forces moved in. The Red Cross building for officers was down near the bottom of the Via Veneto at the Piazza Barberini, and it served as the advantageous assembling point for those of us from the same squadron there at the same time who wished for a breakfast, lunch, or snack of familiar food at prices we could easily afford before taking off for our roamings about the incredible and exciting city of Rome. The memories of the time held by Jean are different from mine, and our experiences of course differ, too. For me and other servicemen there on leave, it was a peaceful place of opulent multiple pleasures; for Jean and her family, existing under the successive occupations of the Germans and the Allies, it was a time of uncertainty and hardship, with indelible memories of fear, cold, curfews, poverty, civic violence between opposing civilian political factions, shortages of food, and long lines for water—water not just for washing but for drinking, too.

The long-term effects, if any, upon our respective personalities are the reverse of what you might expect. She is a person of unflagging good cheer who never seems to cease smiling, working, and laughing; while I, I've been told, am given to much unconscious frowning and scowling while alone in contemplative silence, even when alone on a lounge chair in the succoring sunshine on one of the spacious decks of Villa d'Este.

Her first meaningful occupation as an adult was doing publicity work in Rome for TWA, Trans World Airlines. The transition from coffee and doughnuts for the Red Cross to the public and customer relations representative in Italy for an international airline does not seem a simple sequence, but Jean appears to have made the progression smoothly and competently. Frequently, she was called to New York for meetings and news briefings on company policies, where she broadened her English and established new friendships that survive to this day, including a few with people who have in the past been acquaintances of mine. But her tact and intelligence were her own. She has related to me the occasion of her escorting about Rome an American

of notable position (she did not disclose his name and I did not ask) who, contemplating the vista of the glorious city from a high place, asked which way he would have to look to see the Acropolis.

"Oh, you cannot see the Acropolis from here," she answered pleasantly. "It's too far away, and we haven't the time today to go there."

A day or so later, he phoned from Athens to compliment her laughingly for the diplomacy with which she had handled his mistaken question.

In time, she married and moved with her husband and children to Milan, where she established a sound reputation doing public relations and publicity work. And more than 30 years ago, in 1967, when the present management of Villa d'Este decided to restore, modernize, and enhance the elegance of the grounds, buildings, and facilities, they sensibly sought her services to celebrate and make known the enrichments, and she has been with Villa d'Este ever since.

A history like hers definitely qualifies her for the compilation of a history like this one (if in doubt, open the book once more to any page for a quick look at the illustrations and the text), of the magnificent site and charming appointments, and of the succession of occupants extending from Countess Caroline of Brunswick to the streams of present-day guests, who, arriving for the first time, beam with looks of an enchanted disbelief that do not lessen from one day to the next. There is delight in all directions, wherever the eye falls.

My own perspective tends to be personal, and it was the lavish extent of the buffet breakfast laid out and awaiting me on the first morning of my first stay there that evoked in me a stimulating and creative response. Harboring all my adult life a distaste for physical activ-

ABOVE: AT NIGHT, THE MOSAIC IS ESPECIALLY DRAMATIC.

ity, and having little better in mind to cope with as I lazily sunned myself from one hour to the next on a lounge chair, I began to write sentences for an article centered on that luxuriant buffet, and some months later it was published in the quarterly supplement of *Forbes* magazine called FYI. In it, I wrote as follows:

My initial response to the abundance that greeted my eyes was a kind of bewildered ecstasy, an intoxicated impression of an enormous breakfast room containing a buffet I did not know could exist outside the whimsical visions of novelists with extraordinary powers of description.

In the dazzling cyclorama of edibles I saw (or thought I saw) glittering pans of biscuits and pots of boiled eggs, baskets of breads and sweet buns, kettles of fish, creamers and crocks and gallipots brimming, compotes and hoppers and casseroles steaming, dry cereals in bushels and hot ones in cauldrons, pans and bins of butters, cheeses, jams, and marmalades, platters with fruit tarts and fruit pies and a cake with layers, urns of fresh milk and jugs of milks of other kinds, ewers of yogurts and sweet and sour cream, and condiments in cruets, flagons, and flasks.

There were basins of fruit and bushels of washed small vegetables, and fragrant tureens of cooked compounds I lacked the learning to identify. Glowing brightly like a rubicund Christmas log near the middle of the table was a firkin or two, perhaps a whole kilderkin, of small strawberries, and another firkin or two of wild raspberries. I couldn't wait to get my lips around them.

Alas, I confess now that the whimsical visions of this writer did escort him into some wild exaggerations of detail, but the overall effect was pretty much what I felt then, and have felt each time since.

About the spectacular setting, the décor, and the furnishings, Jean Salvadore has here presented with photographs and text a much better account than I could possibly give. The service is suavely impeccable, as I wrote in the article, and I also remarked on my impression that you "could search the capacious establishment for a stain of rust or chipped spot of paint, and you would probably search in vain."

To Claudio Ceccherelli, now the general manager, just last year I commented upon leaving that Villa d'Este under his supervision quietly creates with subdued charm the confident feeling that one can obtain just about anything one wants there—if one is able to pay for it. He smiled at my afterthought and seemed pleased by the compliment implied in that part, too.

At the time we met, Jean Marc Droulers—who presently is part owner and executive supervisor—had what I guessed was the best view from his house in all Lake Como. I had not been there, but his home was directly across the lake, and I could picture him looking out many times daily through his windows across the blue water to the sumptuous splendor of his establishment, which gleams in daylight and glows with golden electrical illumination at night, and enjoying the most satisfying feeling of proprietorship possible for a human to experience.

Villa d'Este is of course an eminent presence in the organization of the 100 best hotels in the world. Of these, I have been to just a few—one in Capri, one in Positano, and this one on Lake Como. I feel no need for more.　—JOSEPH HELLER, NOVEMBER 1999

preface

A magical experience like Villa d'Este doesn't happen in a day—it takes literally decades to polish and refine, as has been done with such love by generations of owners, managers, and staff since it first opened its doors as a grand hotel on the shores of Lake Como in 1873.

ABOVE: JEAN MARC DROULERS.

Originally established four centuries ago thanks to the drive and vision of Cardinal Gallio, I believe if either he or Caroline of Brunswick could read this book—with its memories and impressions of times and people no longer here—they would be pleased to be at the origins of what Villa d'Este stands for today.

As you may gather, I am very proud of our extended Villa d'Este family, which numbers around 250 people. Just about 70 percent of them have been with us for more than 15 years. I feel privileged working with them, the very best of Italians: a group of men and women of all ages, for whom Villa d'Este is not just a living, but a rewarding way of life in which they take pride. They are attentive, as the great professionals they are, but they feel comfortable with people at every level in a very graceful way. Best of all, they always have a ready smile!

Not least among the people who have made the difference here at Villa d'Este is Jean Salvadore, a remarkable lady whom I have had the honor to count as both a friend and a colleague since I took over more than 24 years ago. (Jean is already the author of two highly successful cookbooks for Villa d'Este, written in collaboration with our chef Luciano Parolari, who has himself been part of the team for 33 years.)

When Jean came to me at the time of our 125th anniversary a few years ago with the idea for a book on Villa d'Este "style," I was immediately intrigued and delighted. Between the two of us, we make up the living memory of Villa d'Este: In my own role, I pride myself also as the guardian of the history of the estate and its atmosphere, belongings, archives—many of which were lost to us forever during the turmoil of World War II—and works of art, both great and small; Jean is the vital link with the history of the people who came here, why they came, the folklore, and the anecdotes—both serious and hilarious—that make up the fabric of daily life in a great hotel. She too is a natural archivist and historian, qualities without which this book could not have been written. We often think of Villa d'Este as theater on a grand scale, where we see things—great characters, sadness, joy, slices of life—both from front of stage and behind the scenes. The fact that Jean has bore witness to all this for more than 33 years is remarkable in itself, but it is her sparkling intelligence and rare insight that give life to the story of *Villa d'Este Style*, as you will see.

Our philosophy here at Villa d'Este is that a hotel is not just a place to sleep and eat along the journey—it has to be a way of life itself. We are concerned not just with the comfort of the body, but of the mind and heart as well. We want to look after every need of the discerning traveler today, yet retain the discreet allure of a private, patrician villa where our guests feel treasured in the old-fashioned way.

That is the future.

I hope that in your own journey through these pages, you will share the same pleasure I took in looking at the past, just for a moment, before moving ahead. —JEAN MARC DROULERS

introduction

Back in the 1950s, I was living in Rome, doing public relations for the airline TWA. When I ventured north to Milan on business, I would always stay in the city—that is, until I discovered Villa d'Este. It was love at first sight!

In 1966, my husband, Luca Salvadore, had the opportunity to become Publisher Angelo Rizzoli's public relations director in Milan. Being a dutiful Italian wife, I reluctantly tagged along, with our son, Andrea, and daughter, Claudia, in tow. After 20 years in the exciting world of travel and tourism, I said goodbye to the Roman *dolce vita* to become a housewife. But not for long...

I suppose it had to be fate; on a glorious sunny day in 1967, I returned to Villa d'Este—no longer as a guest, but as the hotel's public relations consultant.

And coming full circle, Rizzoli Internaional Publications is the publisher of this book.

Long ago, I got into the habit of keeping a diary, noting all the events at the hotel and listing the friends and guests I would meet each day. I realized that this material would be lost unless I did something to preserve it. Friends encouraged me to write a book; when I spoke about it with Jean Marc Droulers, Villa d'Este's C.E.O., he was so enthusiastic that he helped me explore the hotel's archives. This was the most fun part!

In the years that I have been with Villa d'Este, the Droulers family has made many improvements, from the famous floating swimming pool to the world-renowned cuisine. All of these changes have resulted in Villa d'Este being ranked among the top hotels in the world year after year. But one constant is the staff—an utterly loyal group who takes pride in belonging to the Villa d'Este family. Its devotion explains why so many guests consider Villa d'Este their home away from home.

I myself, after 33 heavenly years here, am still mesmerized by the magical atmosphere of this unique corner of paradise. I hope that through this book a bit of this magic reaches you.

OPPOSITE: THE NYMPHAEUM IN THE INTERIOR OF THE MOSAIC.

The precise location of heaven on heart

has never been established

but it may very well be right here.

—HERB CAEN, JULY 1970

OPPOSITE: A VIEW OF BLEVIO ON THE FACING SHORE, SEEN FROM THE TERRACE OF A
SUITE IN THE CARDINAL'S BUILDING

chapter one

the most romantic lake in the world

"this lake exceeds anything i ever beheld in beauty."

— SHELLEY

For over 2,000 years, poets from Virgil and Catullus to Tennyson and Longfellow have raved about the lakes of Lombardy, but it is impossible to do justice when describing the spectacular beauty of Lake Como without a photograph in hand. However, the fact is that the beauty of the lake inspired the English scientist William Henry Fox Talbot to imprint images of the extraordinary Lake Como on paper. Fox Talbot visited Como in October 1833, and upon returning to England in January 1834, he went to work in his laboratory. The memory of Como's beauty drove him on, as did the knowledge that the Frenchman Louis Daguerre was working toward the same goal: the invention of photography. The two men today share the distinction of having invented photography, but Como shares with no other locale the honor of having inspired it.

OPPOSITE: AN AERIAL VIEW OF THE FAMOUS VILLAGE OF BELLAGIO, ALSO LOCATED ON LAKE COMO. EVEN LEONARDO DA VINCI SPENT TIME HERE.

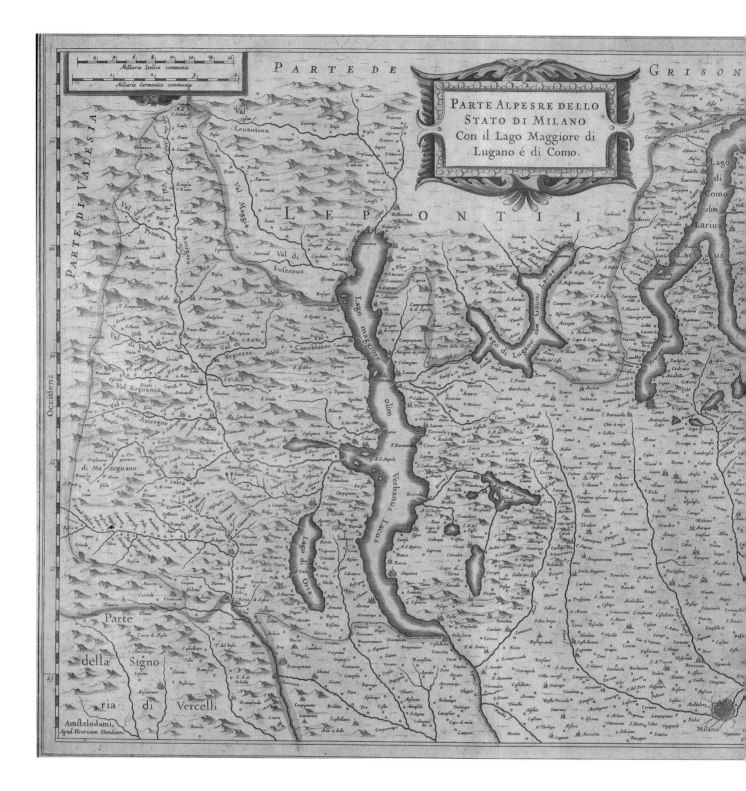

Lake Como was discovered over 2,000 years ago by the Romans, who elected these surroundings as their favored retreat. In 49 B.C., Julius Caesar took charge of Como, populated it with 5,000 "colonists," and named the lake Larius. The most famous sons of Como (then known as *Novum Comum*) were the two Plinys, both born there: Pliny the Elder, author of the celebrated *Natural History* in 37 books; and his nephew, Pliny the Younger, a Latin prose author.

Holiday villas have been popular on Como since the first century A.D., when Pliny the Younger had not one but two villas on the lake—one called Comedy, the other Tragedy. In the 19th century, Longfellow came to Lake Como to write, as did Tennyson. Composer Franz Liszt came here in 1837 and wrote his *Dante Fantasia*; Bellini wrote his opera *Norma*; and the dancer Taglioni lived at Blevio.

LEFT: THE LAKE REGION OF LOMBARDY, CIRCA 1780. BELOW: COMO IS A STONE'S THROW FROM VILLA D'ESTE. ITS HISTORY DATES BACK TO THE PREHISTORIC DAYS. THERE IS A ROMAN COMO, WITH ITS RUINS OF POWERFUL WALLS AND STREET PAVINGS. THERE ARE ALSO MANY REMAINS OF MEDIEVAL COMO, SUCH AS THE 12TH-CENTURY TOWN WALLS AND THE BASILICAS. THE MOST IMPORTANT BUILDING OF RENAISSANCE COMO IS THE CATHEDRAL, SEEN IN THE LEFT OF THE PHOTOGRAPH. VILLA OLMO, ALSO IN COMO, BELONGS TO THE NEOCLASSICAL COMO. MODERN COMO IS REPRESENTED BY THE BUILDINGS OF COMO ARCHITECT GIUSEPPE TERRAGNI.

Until World War II, the lake provided paradise and comfort for the well-heeled. But, when Mussolini and Claretta Petacci, his mistress, were captured at the town of Dongo and shot in nearby Mezzegra in 1945, Italians shied away from Como. Twenty years later, a new crop of the elegant and famous began to move in.

Today, Como has become highly industrialized, but the town has been left intact and unspoiled. Most of the streets remain closed to all but pedestrian traffic. All of the factories are located on the outskirts of Como, which survives as the premier manufacturer of quality silk and textiles in the world.

One of the greatest historic achievements of Como was the formation of the Maestri Comacini (master builders), consisting of builders, stonecutters, and decorators who, for centuries, were in demand all over Italy

when you write of two happy lovers,

let the story be set on the banks of lake como.

—FRANZ LISZT

ABOVE: THE "LUCIA" IS SYMBOLIC OF LAKE COMO AS IS THE GONDOLA OF VENICE. ITS NAME DERIVES FROM THE EARLIEST KNOWN FICTION OF ITALY, *I PROMESSI SPOSI* (THE BETROTHED), WRITTEN BY ALESSANDRO MANZONI. OPPOSITE: ONE OF THE BEST WAYS TO SEE LAKE COMO IS BY BOAT. VARENNA, PICTURED HERE, IS AN UNSPOILED VILLAGE ABOUT TWO HOURS FROM VILLA D'ESTE BY THE LOCAL FERRY, OR 40 MINUTES BY HYDROFOIL. THE MULTI-COLORED CLUTTER OF HOUSES IS SO BECOMING THAT IT IS QUITE BREATHTAKING IN ITS GEN-UINE SIMPLICITY; BUT UPON WALKING ALONG THE "PASSEGGIATA," ONE WILL BE SURPRISED TO SEE THAT THERE IS A CHOICE THAT SPANS VISITS TO TRATTORIAS, FANCY RESTAURANTS, CHARMING HOTELS, AND STYLISH STORES, AS IS TO BE EXPECTED IN A SEASIDE RESORT THAT IS RELATIVELY UNDISCOVERED BY MANY TOURISTS.

LEFT: THE CATHEDRAL OF COMO IS A BLEND OF ARCHITECTURAL STYLES AND PROBABLY THE MOST FAMOUS TOURIST DESTINATION OF THE TOWN OF COMO. BELOW: TORNO, ANOTHER ENCHANTING VILLAGE, SITUATED UP-LAKE AND DIAGONALLY ACROSS FROM VILLA D'ESTE. OPPOSITE: ISOLA COMACINA WAS A MILITARY STRONGHOLD IN CENTURIES LONG PAST AND A CENTER FOR NAVAL BATTLES AGAINST COMO. THE EXCUSE TO VISIT THE ISLAND IS TO ENJOY AN EXCELLENT MEAL IN THE RESTAURANT LOCANDA. OFFERING A SET MENU FOR BOTH LUNCH AND DINNER, DAY IN AND DAY OUT, THE UNUSUAL FEATURE HERE IS THAT NO PASTA IS SERVED. INSTEAD, ONE EATS VEGETABLES TO START, THEN LAKE FISH, CHICKEN, CHEESE, DESSERT, AND A CEREMONIAL COFFEE. ALTHOUGH THE ISLAND IS HANDKERCHIEF-SIZE, IT IS SAID THAT AT ONE TIME IT ACCOMMODATED NINE CHURCHES.

VILLA DEL PIZZO Situated in an ancient place ("in pizz" that is) on the promontory close to Villa d'Este, this site was, even as far back as the 15th century, occupied by a country house. The Comense Mugiasca family erected the villa in the mid- 18th century. After the death of the last owner, the Marchesa Dinetta d'Amico, the villa was opened to the public.

VILLA MELZI This elegant neoclassical construction located in Bellagio is listed as a historic monument. It was originally the summer residence of Napoleon I's vice president of the Italian Republic. Built between 1801 and 1810, of special note are the lakeside walk, the noble chapel, and the museum pavilion containing important archeological findings, Napoleonic relics, and splendid Renaissance frescoes.

VILLA DEL BALBIANELLO The most beaautiful of all Como's villas, this was originalli known as Villa Arconati and is located on the extreme tip of a promontory. It was built by Cardinal Durini in the 18th century and was designated an Italian national trust home in 1988. It houses the museum of the relics of the last owner, Count Guido Monzino, famous for his mountaineering and polar espeditions.

visitors

VILLA CARLOTTA *The most famous historical villa is Villa Carlotta, which dates back more than two centuries. Its name derives from the fact that is given as a wedding gift by Princess Marianne of Prussia to her daughter Carlotta. It now belongs to the Italian state and is notable for its museum and garden, which has a rich botanical patrimony noted especially for its azaleas.*

VILLA OLMO *Built in 1782 by Innocenzo Odescalchi, since 1926 the villa has been used for important cultural and artistic exhibitions; and since 1982, it has been used as the headquarters for the Alessandro Volta Center. Volta, the inventor of the electric battery, was a friend of Queen Caroline and helped her to purchase Villa d'Este in 1815.*

VILLA ERBA *Built in 1892 by Carlo Erba, a wellknown pharmaceutical industrialist, it was passed down to his grandchildren, who included Luchino Visconti. In its lakeside position, surrounded by a parkland, this villa is the last beacon of a lost generation. It is a perfect setting for important occasions, exhibitions, and high-level meetings.*

and Europe. The Maestri helped Como to become one of the wealthiest provinces of Italy. This affluence is one of the primary reasons that Como is enjoyable for visitors; tourism is not considered its main financial resource. In fact, the major financial invigorators of Como are its textiles industry and furniture manufacture and design, with the tourism industry following a distant third. This has kept Como from being overbuilt with high-rises, so that even during the peak of the season, the lake does not appear to be crowded.

The secret to visiting and understanding Como is to travel the region by boat. Every building on the shore, old and new, from a Hemingway shack to a Dutch doll's house or a Lusitanian Gothic, is designed to be seen from the water, affording splendid opportunities to peer into idiosyncratic "front rooms." Most of the smaller houses on the waterfront are second homes for wealthy citizens from Milan, which is less than an hour away.

The lake is approximately 28 miles (45 km) long and never more than 2 miles (3km) wide, so both shores are always visible from either side or the middle. Private boats and ferries travel up and down the lake, offering views of the most important villas, such as Villa d'Este and Villa del Balbianello, so beautifully described by Edith Wharton in her 1904 classic book *Italian Villas and Their Gardens*. Some other important villas include Villa Pizzo, Versace's Villa Fontanelle, Villa Pliniana, and Villa Carlotta.

From the pier of the scenic town of Cernobbio, a less-than-two-hour boat ride transports visitors to Bellagio, "Pearl of the Lake"—the most picturesque village on Lake Como. Bellagio is an idyllic miniature town with striped mooring poles and steep cobbled alleys, restaurants, grand hotels, and quayside shops. Best of all, Bellagio has views: of the desolate northern reaches of the lake, with alpine peaks above smaller, granular mountains; of the ranks of villas and gardens hemming the sunny southern arm of the lake, which runs south to the busy town of Como; and of irregular green hills and haphazard mountain ranges that define the millpond lake to the west and east.

Cernobbio, located three miles from the town of Como, remained an obscure hamlet populated only by fishermen and woodcutters until the 15th century. In 1442, a handful of nuns took refuge in a small convent known as the Cloister of Sant' Andrea, which is today the site of Villa d'Este's park.

> At eventide, when everything seems to slumber and the music of the vesper bells come stealing over the water, one almost believes that nowhere else than on the Lake of Como can there be found such a paradise of tranquil repose.
>
> —MARK TWAIN, *THE INNOCENTS ABROAD*

OPPOSITE, TOP: THE CELEBRATED VILLA PLINIANA. THE NAME "PLINIANA" WAS GIVEN TO THE VILLA BECAUSE OF THE INTERMITTENT WATERFALL—WHICH IS ABOUT 260 FEET (80 METERS) HIGH AND CAN BE SEEN ONLY FROM THE VILLA OR FROM THE LAKE—AS DESCRIBED BY THE TWO PLINYS. IT IS SAID THAT LEONARDO DA VINCI PAID A VISIT BECAUSE HE WAS INTRIGUED BY THIS PHENOMENON OF NATURE. ITS INTERMITTENCE IS NOW EXPLAINED BY THE SYPHON STRUCTURE OF THE ROCK FROM WHICH IT GUSHES. OPPOSITE, BOTTOM: A VIEW OF THE CITY OF COMO AT SUNSET WITH A FLEET OF SAILBOATS IN THE FOREGROUND AND THE DOME OF THE CATHEDRAL IN THE BACKGROUND.

TODAY, VILLA D'ESTE FINDS ITSELF ON THE OUTSKIRTS OF THE VILLAGE OF CERNOBBIO, ORIGINALLY
CALLED *COENOBIUM* BY THE ROMANS. IT WAS A FISHING VILLAGE UNTIL THE CARDINAL BUILT HIS

VILLA GARROVO, THE CURRENT VILLA D'ESTE, IN 1568. OPPOSITE: EARLY MORNING ENVELOPS THE LAKESHORE OF CERNOBBIO. ABOVE: THE PIER OF CERNOBBIO, WHERE BOATS ARRIVE AND DEPART.

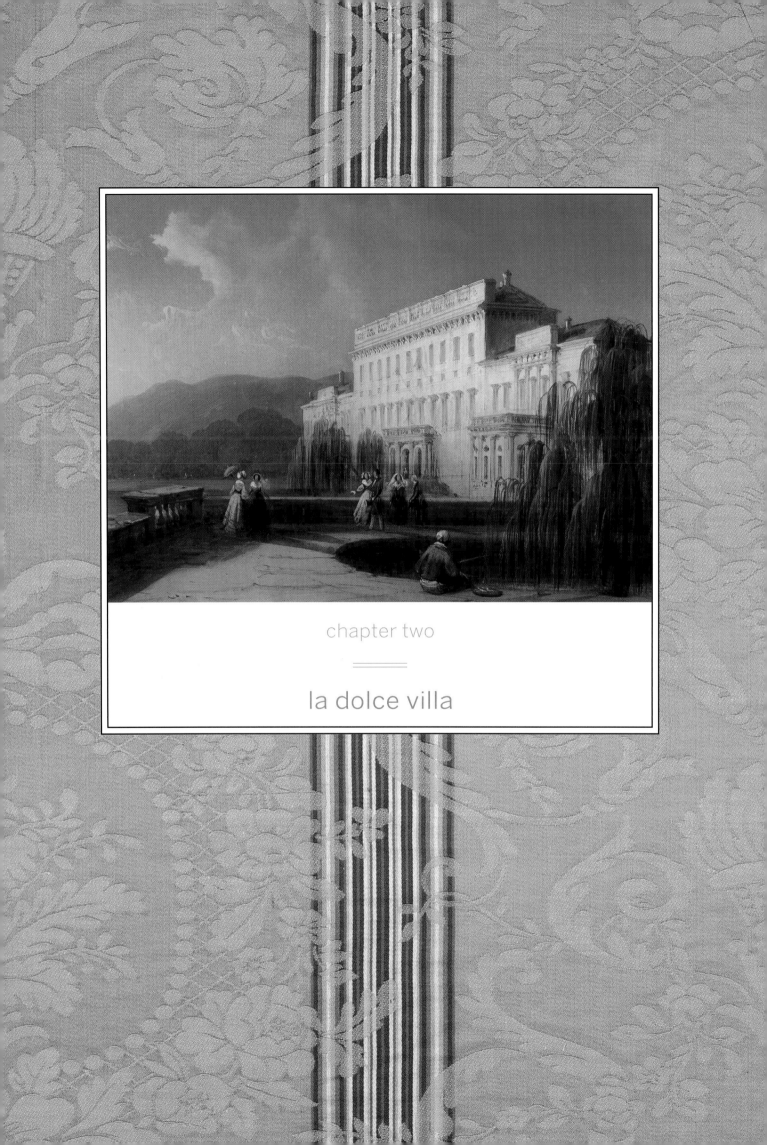

chapter two

la dolce villa

"here everything is noble and touching, everything speaks of love."

— STENDHAL

The history of Villa d'Este dates back over 500 years to when Cernobbio was a little village. First to arrive on the site where the hotel compound now stands were the nuns who took refuge from the Civil War in a church where the park of Villa d'Este is located today. By the middle of the 15th century, a convent was added and the name "Cloister of Sant' Andrea" was given to it. Some of the columns that exist in the park today are said to have belonged to the nunnery.

It was not until a century later that the actual villa was built. One of the leading families of the period was the Ottavio Gallios, the parents of three sons; the youngest, Tolomeo, studied in Rome and returned to Como as a cardinal of the city at the age of 38, under the papacy of Pius IV. At this time, the Gallios, having acquired the old Cloister of Sant' Andrea and an extension of surrounding land, decided to build a villa on the lake's shore, which at the time was considered extremely fashionable. One of the best architects of the day, Pellegrino Pellegrini of Valsolda, was commissioned by Cardinal Tolomeo Gallio to do the planning.

OPPOSITE: AN EARLY-19TH-CENTURY VIEW OF VILLA D'ESTE SHOWING THE HOTEL BEFORE THE TERRACE WAS BUILT. THE ONLY WAY TO REACH THE PROPERTY WAS BY WATER.

The villa, named Garrovo, was built in 1568 and was considered one of the finest examples of architecture and landscaping at the time. In addition to acting as secretary of state at the Vatican and dean of the Sacred College, Cardinal Tolomeo Gallio was also a noted patron of arts and letters; the country mansion soon became a gathering place for the elite, who were royally entertained whenever the high prelate of the church was in residence. After the cardinal's death, Villa Garrovo was inherited by a nephew, Tolomeo, duke of Alvito, who continued to embellish the house and gardens in true Renaissance style.

For over two centuries, the House of Gallio reigned uncontested on the shores of Cernobbio. During the latter part of the 18th century, one of the descendants of Tolomeo Gallio moved to Naples and the family began to lose interest in the property. The house and land were more or less abandoned. A Jesuit order retreated here, and the villa and, consequently, Cernobbio, fell into oblivion for many years until the advent of the Napoleonic empire.

In 1782, Carlo Tolomeo Gallio Trivulzio, duke of Alvito, sold the estate to Count Ruggero Marliani, colonel of the Austrian army and delegate to the government of Lombardy; but only two years later, the villa had a new proprietor: the Marquis Bartolomeo Calderara. A dissolute and affluent aristocrat who squandered a fortune on wine, women, and song, he qualified as a real *signore* because he never had to work for a living, meaning that he had the reputation of a gentleman.

Despite being an aged Milanese playboy, the renovation of Villa Garrovo was due to Calderara, who had married Vittoria Peluso, a ballerina nicknamed "Pelusina." It was rumored that the marchioness was not accepted by the aristocracy of Milan because she

LEFT: CARDINAL TOLOMEO GALLIO, WHO IS TODAY KNOWN AS A MAN OF LETTERS, ENTERTAINED HIS LITERARY FRIENDS AT HIS VILLA, NAMED GARROVO, BUILT IN 1568. ABOVE: COUNT DOMENICO PINO, A NAPOLEONIC GENERAL WHOSE WIFE, TO KEEP HIM AMUSED, BUILT THE FORTIFICATIONS THAT TODAY OVERLOOK THE GROUNDS OF VILLA D'ESTE. OPPOSITE: REMAINS OF THE ANCIENT CLOISTER OF SANT' ANDREA.

was a social climber. (In those days, a marriage between an aristocrat and a ballerina, even a famous one, created quite a scandal in the so-called high society. It was unheard of for a nobleman to wed a commoner, even though Pelusina pirouetted on the La Scala stage.) The marchioness ignored the slight and undertook an ambitious plan of building up her image in the eyes of the noble families of Lombardy.

The marchioness decided to abandon Palazzo Calderara in Milan, choosing to live on Lake Como in Villa Garrovo. She moved to Cernobbio and dedicated her time and her husband's wealth to restoring the villa to its past splendor. She did this with great taste and distinction, under the guidance of her spouse, who taught Vittoria all there was to know about savoir faire. The gardens were perfected and the interiors were redone in a grand style.

Once the old marquis died, Donna Vittoria, still young and attractive, immediately remarried. She chose as her husband a Napoleonic general, Count Domenico Pino. (Napoleon had shown a predilection for the valorous Pino and named him count.)

In 1815, the most famous resident of Villa d'Este (then still Villa Garrovo) made her entrance: Caroline of Brunswick-Wolfenbuttel, Princess of Wales and future Queen of England. Her residence was undoubtedly the most interesting chapter in the history of the villa, which she renamed "New Villa d'Este." Many controversial books have been written about the tragic figure Caroline, and many slanderous things were said. One thing that cannot be contested is that she spent the happiest time of her troubled life on Lake Como.

Caroline, as Princess of Wales, lived virtually in exile at Villa d'Este. She left her marriage to the Prince of Wales, later George IV, King of England, after only 18 days, traveling throughout Europe without a residence. When she discovered Lake Como in 1814, it was love at first sight.

Determined to purchase the estate of Garrovo, Caroline rented a villa in Como. The following year, Countess Pino consented to the sale. (The Pinos took up residence in Villa Cima, which is the first house one passes on the right after entering the gates of Villa d'Este.) Princess Caroline changed the name to "New Villa d'Este." The connection with the Este family was very remote, but through research it was found that the House of Brunswick, to which Caroline belonged, and the House of Hanover, from which her estranged husband descended, both originated from a certain Guelfo d'Este, who left Germany for Italy in 1504. The name held, but the addition of "new" to avoid confusion with the Villa d'Este in Tivoli, near Rome, was soon dropped.

For five years Caroline d'Este completely dedicated herself to further adorning and decorating her beloved residence. She created a magnificent library and a theater for festivals, comedies, and tragedies. She hired a team of architects and painters to redecorate the rooms and placed the famed statue *Venus Crowned by Eros* (attributed to Canova) in her private apartments.

In 1820, Caroline returned to London in an abortive attempt to take her place on the throne, leaving the Villa d'Este deed of sale in the hands of her banker with the understanding that she could get it back by paying her debts. But Caroline was never to return. She died heartbroken in 1821 after the scandalous divorce

OPPOSITE: A PORTRAIT OF PRINCESS CAROLINE OF BRUNSWICK (1768-1821) PAINTED BY SIR THOMAS LAWRENCE. JANE AUSTEN DESCRIBED PRINCESS CAROLINE, THE ESTRANGED WIFE OF GEORGE IV, AS "BAD, BUT SHE WOULD NOT HAVE BECOME AS BAD AS SHE WAS IF HE HAD NOT BEEN INFINITELY WORSE."

action filed against her by the king. At Villa d'Este, a long period of neglect followed.

Vittorina, the daughter of Caroline's lover, the charmer Bartolomeo Pergami, should have inherited the estate, according to the Princess's will. Yet the legalities were never worked out: Prince Torlonia, the banker, became the owner, as he was still in possession of the deed of sale. However, nobody resided at the villa, and it was completely abandoned.

In 1829, the heirs of Prince Torlonia sold the property to Prince Domenico Orsini. He in turn sold it to Baron Ippolito Ciani in 1834, who began restoring the estate with loving care, including replacing the yellowed tapestry in the Napoleon Room.

His most important change to the estate was the building of a new villa named in honor of Caroline: Hotel de la Reine d'Angleterre. (The plan was to launch it as a spa, but this failed.) Overlooking the lake and located beyond the landmark 500-year-old plane tree

that still stands today, the building is a trompe l'oeil masterpiece now known as the Queen's Pavilion.

Ciani sold the totally rehabilitated estate to a group of ingenious businessmen who formed a limited company known as Villa d'Este and combined into one property the two villas: The Cardinal's Building and the Queen's Pavilion. The year of the birth of the estate as a hotel was in 1873. Once again, architects and engineers moved in to build a terrace overlooking the lake where the façade of the villa originally rose directly out of the water.

Since that time, Villa d'Este has experienced constant renovations and additions, including a golf course, dining rooms serving world-class cuisine, tennis courts, a sporting club, spa, watersport activities, and continual updating of the guest rooms with authentic period furnishings and fabrics. All of these things help to make Villa d'Este much more than a hotel. Yet every aspect of the luxury and magnificence of bygone eras is still intact; only now all the modern comforts are included as well.

"Returning Justice lifts aloft her Scale"
Pope

Travelling Tête à Tête !!
"Ha, Ha, by Gar vat dat I see yonder,
Dat look so tempting red and vite?"

The Modern Genius of History at her Toilet,
Dressing for a Masquerade. Having assistance Boys and
See the chaste Historic Muse. Feathers, gause chemise and shoes.

The Como-cal Hobby.
Set a Courier on Goat-back and he'll ride to the Devil.

OPPOSITE AND ABOVE: A SERIES OF CARICATURES THAT RELATE THE STORY OF THE "LADY AND THE MAITRE DE PLAISIR," WHICH DISCREDITS THE FUTURE QUEEN, CAROLINE OF BRUNSWICK. EACH CARTOON FEATURES CAROLINE, THINLY DISGUISED IN AN UNFLATTERING LIGHT, WITH HER CHAMBERLAIN, BARTOLOMEO PERGAMI. NOTE VILLA D'ESTE SEEN IN THE BACKGROUND OF THE FIRST AND LAST DRAWINGS ON THIS PAGE.

[1815]   [1847]

IMAGES OF VILLA D'ESTE FROM EARLY DAYS UNTIL THE PRESENT.

[1955]   [2000]

THE MAIN BUILDING HAS MAINTAINED ITS ESSENTIAL CHARACTER THROUGH TIME.

45

chapter three

the mosaic, the plane tree,
and the garden

"i ask myself is this a dream; will it vanish into air?"

—LONGFELLOW

"In the gardens of the Villa d'Este there is much of the Roman spirit—the breadth of design, the unforced inclusion of natural features, and that sensitivity to the quality of the surrounding landscape. Behind the Villa d'Este, the mountains are sufficiently withdrawn to leave a gentle acclivity," wrote Edith Wharton. This "gentle acclivity" that she describes accommodates the central axis of the garden, placed alongside the villa so that the view to and from the lake remains open and clear.

The garden consists of a large parterre that is divided into four squares and is set back from the lakeshore. The statue of Hercules, set inside a rotunda above the lake, steeply descends to the nymphaeum located in the middle

OPPOSITE: THE GROUNDS OF VILLA D'ESTE ARE ONE OF ITS MOST COMPELLING FEATURES. HERE IS A CONTEMPLATIVE NICHE, THE TEMPLE OF TELEMACHUS, TUCKED INTO THE ASCENDING HILLSIDE EN ROUTE TO THE HERCULES STATUE.

of the famous mosaic. Today, the superb double-water staircase from the Hercules downward is one of the few surviving fragments of the original garden built in 1568 by Tolomeo Gallio. Gallio's landscape architect was Pellegrino Pellegrini—painter, sculptor, architect —and, most important, a follower of Renaissance genius Michelangelo.

At this time, architects working in Rome demonstrated their infatuation with Imperial Rome by designing gardens that were reflective of its principles. Because Pliny was born in Como, Pellegrino Pellegrini made further use of the association between Imperial Rome and Villa d'Este: A group of plane trees, a species greatly admired by Pliny, was planted by the edge of the water while his favorite ivy was used decoratively to swathe the stonework and as garlands.

Unusual, however, for a garden of such pronounced Roman influence is the off-center relationship of the water staircase to the villa. It is thought that Pellegrino Pellegrini intended that the outstanding view of the lake not be obstructed. As a result, the visitor approaching by water could gaze straight up the long "Avenue of the Cypresses" (now containing magnolia trees, too) to the nymphaeum at the summit.

In 1794, when the Marquis Calderara and his wife, La Pelusina, settled in Como, they initiated the next stage in the garden's development. They are the ones who planted the avenue of cypresses and built the mosaic, a grotto, and the Neoclassical temple to house the Hercules atop the hill. And, of course, it was La Pelusina who built the battlements that dot the hillside above Villa d'Este as a playground for her second husband, a returning Napoleonic warrior. Made of cement, the battlements continue to draw crowds who engage in mock warfare, as well as the more passive hikers and view-seekers.

When Caroline of Brunswick moved in at the beginning of the 19th century and renamed the villa New Villa d'Este, she was naming it after Guelfo d'Este, an ancestor whom she had recently discovered she shared with her husband. Guelfo had left Germany in 1504 and joined the court of Cardinal Ippolito I d'Este of Ferrara, to which the fabled Ariosto also belonged. In his honor, Princess Caroline immediately replaced the statue of Hercules at the head of the cascade with that of Ariosto. (During the period of Italy's reunification, the villa was the headquarters for anti-Austrian activity. To downplay their patriotism in the face of the enemy, the owners removed Ariosto, replacing it with one of Hercules flinging the dying Lichas.)

Caroline is responsible for the road that runs through the property today—linking Cernobbio and

Moltrasio—the first road to run along the lakeside. She named the street "La Strada Carolina." (It is now known as "via Regina.") The greatest restorer and builder of the gardens in the history of the villa, Princess Caroline wrote to Lady Charlotte Campbell in 1817 from Villa d'Este: "I should be happy to see you in my little nutshell, which is pretty and comfortable and my gardens are *charmant*. I lead a quiet rural life and work the gardens myself, which do my body and mind good."

Edith Wharton describes the bosco—the landscape of natural woodland climbing the cliffside with winding paths beyond the formal gardens—as "one of the most enchanting bits of sylvan gardening in Italy."

Caroline built a theater as well, where she put on Italian operas in which she herself would perform.

But Caroline's activities paled in comparison to those of her estranged husband, George IV, through his agents in Italy. Given the task of catching Caroline in a compromising position with her lover, Bartolomeo Pergami, or

ABOVE LEFT: THE MOSAIC FROM THE CENTRAL GROUNDS OF THE HOTEL, LOOKING TOWARD THE HERCULES STATUE. ABOVE RIGHT: A DETAIL OF THE INTRICATE STONE-WORK THAT HAS MADE THE MOSAIC FAMOUS, BUILT AS AN ORNAMENT AND STILL PRE- SERVED IN ITS ORIGINAL STRUC- TURE. BOTTOM RIGHT: THE VIEW OF THE GROUNDS FROM THE STEPS OF THE MOSAIC.

jasmine wysteria olive cypress azalea

magnolia hydrangea begonia rose palm

THE FOUR SEASONS
OF THE PLANE TREE.

bribing others to say that they had so that he could divorce her, George IV had spies using the gardens as hiding places. Finally, when Caroline could take it no longer, she sought refuge, returning to England in 1820 to attempt to take her rightful position as Queen of England. But George IV would not allow it. He had Caroline tried for adultery, even bringing her gardeners to London to testify against her. Finally, she was acquitted, but not after prolonged court proceedings and tabloid public scandal. Her death shortly thereafter was quite possibly caused by the strain of it all.

One of the last tenants of Villa d'Este, the Russian empress Maria Federowna, rented the villa in 1868, at which time she opened the gardens to the public. On those days, she had herself rowed onto Lake Como, while swathed in sable and cashmere, as visitors were treated to a puppet show.

The two most memorable features of the glorious gardens today are the mosaic and the one plane tree remaining from the stand of plane trees that existed in the villa's earliest days. The plane tree has become a symbol of the ongoing life at Villa d'Este—the one in the central garden is 500 years old. No matter what the season, the plane tree is majestic, providing a natural counterpoint to all the man-made magnificence of the place.

IN THE EARLY 20TH CENTURY, A FAMILY TAKES A WALK IN THE PARK UNDER THE ROSE ARCHWAY.

ABOVE: THE DOUBLE-WATER STAIRCASE, ONE OF THE FEW REMAINING ORIGINAL FEATURES OF VILLA D'ESTE. OPPOSITE, TOP: THE WATER STAIRCASE ORIGINATES AT THE TOP OF THE HILL WHERE HERCULES, DYING AND MADDENED WITH PAIN, HURLS HIS COMPANION, LICHAS, INTO THE WATERS BELOW. RIGHT: VINTAGE VILLA D'ESTE, CIRCA 1890

chapter four

the pools, the walks – a retreat to luxury

"there is a lake, a swimming pool, and a swimming pool in the lake."

—G.Y. DRYANSKY,
CONDÉ NAST TRAVELER

Man-made elements for sporting enjoyment have been typical of Villa d'Este from the time that it was initiated as a retreat for the Romans. Of course, all outdoor activities have been created to work in conjunction with the natural environment, and it is precisely for this reason that they have been so successful throughout time. As a retreat, whether as a private home or as a hotel for guests, Villa d'Este has been designed to delight, always using the landscape as foil and co-conspirator of outdoor activity and recreational events.

OPPOSITE: THE QUEEN'S PAVILION, THE SECOND BUILDING OF THE CURRENT VILLA D'ESTE COMPLEX, WAS ORIGINALLY BUILT AS A SPA IN 1856 AND NAMED AFTER QUEEN CAROLINE. THE MAIN BUILDING, CALLED THE CARDINAL'S BUILDING, WAS CONSTRUCTED IN 1568.

The fortresses built by the Marchesa Calderara, Vittoria Peluso, are the most prominent and historic evidence of this. Upon acquiring her second husband, the young, handsome Napoleonic general Count Domenico Pino, and fearing that he would suffer separation anxiety on his return from war, "La Pelusina" had a series of simulated fortresses and towers—akin to those in which her husband had fought in Spain—built on the slopes overlooking the gardens. (They still stand today.) Count Domenico Pino was so delighted with the battlements that he recruited a group of military cadets to play mock battles after which elaborate meals were served, capped by fireworks.

Today, the paths through the fortress grounds are used more for strolling than for practice warfare. They provide an incredible maze of paths through which hikes and walks can take hours—or even days. But strolling is only one of the outdoor activities that has made Villa d'Este an international draw. Now there's swimming, motorboating, and tennis to capture the imagination and physical health of its visitors.

Caroline of Brunswick, the most notable private owner of Villa d'Este, spent incredible amounts of money on the villa and its grounds when she was in residence. In fact, her expenses were so extreme that when she died in England, having left the villa only "temporarily" to claim her place as queen, the villa reverted to her bankers, who were owed a fortune. But sadly, there is little indication about exactly what kind of outdoor accoutrements—other than the gardens—she initiated during her time. We do know that in the gossip columns of her day, she was reputed to have been throwing orgies and wild parties. But it seems that these don't really qualify as recreation as we would consider it today!

It is probably the point at which the villa actually became a hotel—in 1873—that real attention was paid to providing activities for visitors that went beyond lolling by the lakeside and consuming five-star meals. Boating was likely the first sporting activity that was encouraged by the consortium of astute businessmen that acquired the villa at this time; but even this was rather a passive endeavor, and it is unlikely that visitors piloted their own crafts. In those days, guests would have arrived with a retinue of servants, and it is likely one or more of them would have steered the craft, hoisted the sails, and seen to the maximum comfort of the guests onboard. Picnics and outdoor dining were also events of the day, but the only exertion here was the lifting of fork to mouth; again, the servants or the hotel staff would have prepared all the foodstuffs.

It was at the turn of the 20th century that sporting activities began to get underway at Villa d'Este, until reaching the crescendo of athletic paradise that one finds here today. A terrace and docks were installed, from which boating activities like rowing and sailing could originate. Two clay tennis courts were added. (Today there are eight hidden in the upper part of the magnificent 18th-century park, above the mosaic.) And visitors became more adventurous, bathing in the cold

LEFT, TOP: THE UNIQUE FLOATING SWIM-MING POOL, ADDED IN 1966, CREATED A SENSATION AND POSSIBLY REMAINS THE ONLY FLOATING POOL IN THE WORLD. LEFT, BOTTOM: POOLGOERS CONTINUE TO BE MESMERIZED BY THE BEAUTY OF LAKE COMO. BELOW, TOP: TENNIS COURTS NOW NUMBER EIGHT ON THE PROPERTY, AS VISITORS ADD SPORTS TO THEIR LEISURE ACTIVITIES. BELOW, BOTTOM: THE QUEEN'S PAVILION, WITH ITS GORGEOUS TROMPE L'OEIL FAÇADE AND UNIQUELY DESIGNED INTERIOR ROOMS, OFFERS VISITORS THE BEST VIEWS OF VILLA D'ESTE'S GROUNDS, THE LAKE, AND ITS ENVIRONS. ITS ROMAN-TIC ATMOSPHERE MAKES IT A FAVORITE FOR HONEYMOONERS.

OPPOSITE: EVEN IN 1934, WHEN THIS PHOTOGRAPH WAS TAKEN, SUNBATHING WAS A MAJOR ACTIVITY AT VILLA D'ESTE

PREVIOUS PAGE: THE CARDINAL'S BUILDING,
THE ORIGINAL STRUCTURE OF VILLA D'ESTE,
IS NOW JUST PART OF THE COMPLEX THAT
COMPRISES BOTH THIS BUILDING AND THE
QUEEN'S PAVILION. ABOVE: A VIEW OF THE
HOTEL FROM THE HILLSIDE FORTIFICATIONS
BUILT FOR COUNT DOMENICO PINO IN 1808.
RIGHT: THE FORTIFICATIONS CONTINUE TO
TANTALIZE VISITORS YOUNG AND OLD ALIKE.
BUILT INTO THE MOUNTAINSIDE ADJACENT TO
THE GARDENS, THEY PROVIDE GREAT WALKING
TERRAIN AND EXTRAORDINARY VIEWS OF THE
HOTEL AND ITS SURROUNDINGS.

but invigorating waters of Lake Como. At this time, Villa d'Este was known as a spa, for it was said that there were natural springs throughout the property that offered waters with special curative powers. But this was a very different spa from the one that graces the main building today, replete with shiatsu, reflexology, and power peels.

Probably the most important architectural modification to affect recreation in the entire history of the villa was the installation of the famous heated floating swimming pool in 1966. At the time, owner Marc Droulers had the foresight to realize that people wanted to not only swim, but sunbathe, too. Without a beach, this was impossible, for the edge of the grounds drops off sharply into Lake Como. He designed a swimming pool that is still unique to the region and probably also to the world. It is a gargantuan pool that is surrounded by a deck for lounging. The swimming pool complex also includes a children's pool with its own private sandy beach. But the main pool is more than just a swimming pool. The structure, supported by pontoons, provides an incredible element of elegance and glamour to the grounds. Lit at night by a thousand tiny bulbs, it fits perfectly with the environment, rather than fighting it, as one might expect. In true Villa d'Este style, the addition is completely in keeping with its surrounding environment and landscape.

Today, the tastes of travelers have changed enormously from those in years gone by. No longer content to loll and gaze at the lake from the terrace all day long, vacationers expect to be occupied from very early in the morning until well past a civilized bedtime. And Villa d'Este offers it all. Besides the putting green on the property itself, there are eight golf courses in the vicinity. One, only seven miles away, is considered one of the finest and most challenging courses ever constructed. The championship links wind over slopes and valleys amidst luxuriant woods along the charming Lake of Montorfano, with scenery similar to the Northern European countries.

A jogging route with 15 checkpoints winds through the grounds above the mosaic. There is also a fully equipped spa, which was inaugurated in 1999 and offers the most up-to-date hydrotherapeutic equipment. In the Sporting Club, visitors can wile away the hours in the fitness center, consisting of a gymnasium, a sauna, Turkish baths, and an indoor swimming pool. Plus, there is a squash court and an electronic golf simulator. Water sports—from motorboating and canoeing to sailing and waterskiing—can be enjoyed in the glorious setting of the pre-Alpine mountains. There is even an underground garage for those visitors who engage in coursing the winding roads alongside Lake Como in fast-moving vehicles as sport. And then of course there is the nightclub—often featuring live music—where one can dance away those calories acquired during a five-course meal at the hotel.

When writer Jean Rafferty posed to herself the question, "Is Villa d'Este grand?" She answered, "Absolutely. But grandeur here is surprisingly seductive." And for those who don't want to partake in any of these grand recreations, there is always the option of sitting on the terrace and watching those who do.

TODAY'S VISITORS TO VILLA D'ESTE ENJOY MORE THAN ITS NATURAL, CULINARY, AND ARCHITECTURAL DELIGHTS. OPPOSITE, TOP: THE SPORTING CLUB, WITH AN EXERCISE ROOM. OPPOSITE, BOTTOM: THE FULL-SIZE SWIMMING POOL. BOTH ARE CONNECTED BY UNDERGROUND PASSAGEWAY TO THE RECENTLY INAUGURATED SPA, OPPOSITE, CENTER.

chapter five

villa b'este

"the italians are so delightfully shameless when it comes to putting on a show."

—TIM PARKS

Many visitors to Villa d'Este plan their trips to the hotel around the series of fetes that take place during the course of the season. People from around the world come not just for the events, but to celebrate them with longstanding guests and friends who return time and again. Particularly popular are the summer parties, planned around events that may include ballet, opera, or concerts. These are staged in the open-air space in front of the mosaic, using the mosaic as the "set" for the event. Stages are erected, professional performers are booked, tables are set, an elaborate menu is planned, and a gala takes place under a starry night.

OPPOSITE: C.E.O. JEAN MARC DROULERS, RIGHT, JOINED BY HIS SON FRANÇOIS, OPENS THE CELEBRATIONS FOR THE 125TH ANNIVERSARY OF VILLA D'ESTE AS A HOTEL BY POURING THE FIRST GLASSES OF CHAMPAGNE ON THE CHAMPAGNE PYRAMID.

Recently, one guest who had attended the "Midsummer Night" party recalled an elegant countess who had assured her over drinks that, "Nothing ever happens at Como." An hour later, the contessa and her tablemate leapt to their feet, both as captivated as children. Dramatically spotlighted over the dark lake, followed by an extravaganza of fireworks, they viewed a ballet of acrobatics: Two dancers on trapezes hung from huge sun and moon balloons. With the trompe l'oeil masterpiece the Queen's Pavilion in the background, the scene was a breathtaking example of the glamour—reminiscent of Cesar Ritz in his heyday—that overtakes Villa d'Este parties. Elegant guests sighed in unison, and another memorable event was posted on the roster of the sublime.

Clearly, entertaining and parties have been a mainstay of the villa since the beginning of its time. The Marchesa Calderara had permanently installed herself and her first husband at Villa d'Este (then Villa Garrovo), having been spurned by the high society of Milan, who had labeled her a "social climber" because of her pedestrian roots. Wanting to prove that she was the queen bee of society, she put most of her effort into entertaining in a grand, cosmopolitan style to put to

THE MOSAIC PROVIDES THE PERFECT BACKDROP FOR WEDDINGS AND DRAWS ROMANTICS FROM AROUND THE WORLD. FEATURED HERE ARE THREE WEDDINGS WITH ALL THE ACCOUTREMENTS.

LEFT: JEAN MARC DROULERS SLICES
THE GORGEOUS CONFECTION PREPARED
BY CHEF LUCIANO PAROLARI TO
CELEBRATE THE HOTEL'S 125TH
ANNIVERSARY. BELOW: HOTEL GUESTS
FLOCK TO ONE OF THE GALA DINNERS
THAT USUALLY INCORPORATE THE
MOSAIC AS A SET FOR THE FESTIVI-
TIES. OPPOSITE: LUCIANO PAROLARI
CREATED THIS ICE SCULPTURE FOR ONE
OF VILLA D'ESTE'S SPECIAL EVENTS.

shame those who had rejected her in Milan. This involved restoring the villa to its past splendor, which she did with great taste and distinction. The villa once again became a "swinging" place, and lavish parties were staged, alternately attended by officers of the French and Austrian armies and the local nobility. Naturally, invitations were sought by even those who had snubbed her earlier.

We know that Caroline of Brunswick not only was famous for her parties, but was criticized because of them. After purchasing the villa in 1815, Caroline dedicated the next five years to adorning and decorating her beloved residence. Although her parties were probably not of the order described in the press to discredit her, there is reason to believe that they were numerous and that they were relatively lively.

In 1834, the most glorious page in the history of Villa d'Este was written, when the villa was acquired by Baron Ippolito Ciani, who had served as aide-de-camp to Napoleon and had been given the title of baron by the emperor. As its owner, he restored the estate with loving care. It was he who built the new villa on the property—then called the Hotel de la Reine d'Angle-terre and now called the Queen's Pavilion—and planned to launch it as a spa.

But more important historically, Milan and all of Lombardy were still under Austrian domination although an insurrection was underway. This is when Villa d'Este underwent another transformation: the return of frivolous parties and banquets. But these were not merely festivities. They were camouflage for the patriotic activities of those involved in the preparation of the Five Days of Milan (March 18-22, 1848) during the period of the Italian Risorgimento, which culminated in 1870 with the unification of Italy. According to legend, the villa became a center of the anti-Austrian movement.

Ippolito Ciani, who descended from a family of manufacturers and bankers, was obliged to entertain high-ranking Austrian officers, so he held all his functions at Villa d'Este. Right under the noses of the enemy, secret meetings would take place. The ladies would hide anti-Austrian pamphlets under their crinolines, the chorus of Verdi's *Nabucco* would be sung, and fireworks would burst into the colors of the Italian flag. It took quite some time for Austrian officials to understand why the composer Giuseppe Verdi had suddenly become so popular that on every occasion the population would break into a chant of "Viva Verdi!" It turned out that this was an acronym for *Viva Vittorio Emanuele Re d'Italia* (Long Live Victor Emanuel, King of Italy!). It is said that Verdi composed his *Traviata* at Villa d'Este, possibly between performances of *Nabucco*, but more likely when he visited as a houseguest of Ciani.

decision to divest, and the villa was sold to investors who would transform it, for the first time, into a hotel.

Today, the hotel not only celebrates cultural and historic events with its lively parties, dining, and entertainment, but because of its gorgeous site it is sought as a location of weddings, anniversaries, family reunions, and other personal events. On some occasions, these festivities are populated with Hollywood glitterati,

The final glamorous page of parties at Villa d'Este was added in 1868, when the Empress Maria Federowna, wife of the Russian czar, rented the villa for a two-month period and stayed on for two years. She was said to entertain in a lively imperial fashion, when not floating in a canopied boat on the lake. Very much admired by the local population because she was kind and dedicated herself to charitable works, her return to Russia caused great sadness in Cernobbio. After the empress was summoned back to the imperial court in 1870, Count Ciani made the

while at other times they are attended by lesser known but equally glamorous citizens of the world. Whatever the occasion, all of the attendees feel that they are part of the event, rather than merely the audience.

Year after year, many of the same guests return to Villa d'Este as if it was their home. This is as much because of the extraordinary entertainment and parties in which staff and guests participate as because of the food and environment. With parties themed to Neapolitan life, Renaissance Italy, a night at La Scala, imperial Vienna, and the Venetian carnival, Villa d'Este offers the magic of another time and place, but it's all here to enjoy now.

chapter six

silk, satin, and statuary

"i recall gentle breezes, cool linen sheets, satin, silk, and silence."

—PAMELA FIORI,
TOWN & COUNTRY

The current aim of Villa d'Este is to recreate the spirit of a classic patrician Italian villa, not a hotel. This is achieved by a stunning synthesis of old-world charm and modern comfort. Most notable of these syntheses is the interior decoration of the Renaissance structure known as the Cardinal's Building and the more recently constructed Queen's Pavilion. Built to delight in 1568 by the best architect of the day, Pellegrino Pellegrini da Valsolda, the Cardinal's Building is not a castle fortress but a Neoclassical palazzo. The red and cream lakeside second building, the Queen's Pavilion, built in 1856 and dedicated by a later

OPPOSITE: THE INTERIOR ARCHITECTURE OF VILLA D'ESTE IS MONUMENTAL. DESIGNED BY ONE OF THE MOST IMPORTANT ARCHITECTS OF THE DAY, PELLEGRINO PELLEGRINI OF VALSOLDA, THE FAME OF VILLA D'ESTE (THEN NAMED VILLA GARROVO AFTER THE MOUNTAIN STREAM THAT FLOWS INTO THE LAKE) REACHED FAR AND WIDE. IN 1615, EVEN THE SULTAN OF MOROCCO—ACCOMPANIED BY HIS COMPLETE RETINUE—ARRIVED IN CERNOBBIO WITH THE SOLE PURPOSE OF VISITING THE VILLA AND SEEING FOR HIMSELF THE REPORTED SPLENDORS.

LEFT: THE ORIGINAL FOYER AS IT APPEARED IN 1930 AND, ABOVE, AS IT APPEARS TODAY. IN 1567, ARCHITECT PELLEGRINO PELLEGRINI WAS COMMISSIONED TO DO THE PLANNING BY CARDINAL TOLOMEO GALLIO. OPPOSITE: TODAY'S CANOVA BAR ENCOMPASSES TWO ROOMS: THE FIRST ROOM (TOP), THE PIANO BAR, DISPLAYS TWO IMPORTANT 16TH-CENTURY ARTWORKS REPRESENTING ADAM AND EVE AND SCULPTED IN CARRARA MARBLE, RESTING IN THE NICHES OF THE ROOM. IT IS BELIEVED THESE WERE SCULPTED

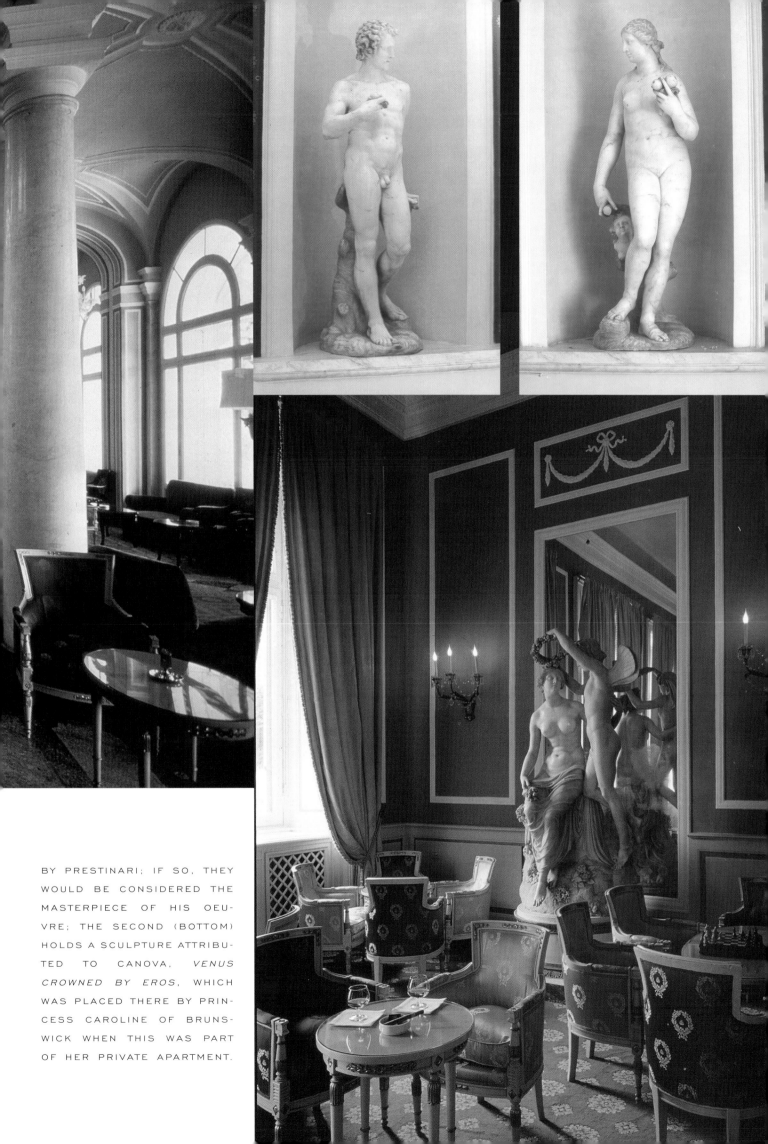

BY PRESTINARI; IF SO, THEY WOULD BE CONSIDERED THE MASTERPIECE OF HIS OEUVRE; THE SECOND (BOTTOM) HOLDS A SCULPTURE ATTRIBUTED TO CANOVA, *VENUS CROWNED BY EROS*, WHICH WAS PLACED THERE BY PRINCESS CAROLINE OF BRUNSWICK WHEN THIS WAS PART OF HER PRIVATE APARTMENT.

owner to former resident Princess Caroline of Brunswick, boasts the same architectural delights as its companion: balconies, terraces, and superb lake views.

Under the creative interior decoration of Roberta Droulers, Villa d'Este interiors are as impressive as their historical housings. Roberta uses as her guide the spirit she has found in the beautiful old houses on the lake. She has individually decorated each of the 133 rooms in the Cardinal's Building and 33 in the Queen's Pavilion with an inviting mix of antique Italian furniture and oil paintings.

Custom-ordered fabrics—silk, velvet, damask, linen, and cotton prints—are used, coming from the grand textile design houses of Ratti and Mantero in Como, Rubelli in Venice, Braquenie in France, and Colefax and Fowler in England. Large marble bathrooms and walk-in wardrobes further underpin the romantic décor. "When I arrive in a room, I want to feel warmth," Roberta says. "One can't put small personal objects in a hotel, so I play with color to give each room character."

In one suite, she has chosen a palette of taupe, in another violet and Moroccan yellow; all shades, including her favorites—turquoise, sage green, and peacock blue—are mixed on the spot for each room and are chosen to work with the light of the lake. Nothing is overdone, and this understated and personalized luxury sets the tone for the stay.

The public spaces in the hotel are equally splendid. The entrance hall, a famous landmark, is replete with blue velvet sofas and empire fauteuils upholstered in blue and gold silk, situated under vaulted ceilings hung with shimmering Venetian chandeliers. Each hallway throughout the hotel has been individually appointed with period couches, tables, and lighting. But all is understated; there's no fussiness here.

The rooms have inspired artists and creative types for centuries. One recent visitor remembers, "Just before dinner, I stood under the arcades watching the mist rise over the lake. The atmosphere was fantastic: The piano was playing, the smell of jasmine was everywhere. I was so inspired that I wrote the first chapter of my novel here."

Artistic inspiration is a consistent theme of Villa d'Este. There is the story of Helmut Newton and his landmark work *White Women*, which was photographed in part at Villa d'Este. In his book he says, "Ever since I was a young boy I've always been fascinated by hotels and hotel rooms. For many years I've taken a great number of my fashion photos in these palaces. Villa d'Este is a place with the most sensuous surroundings and fascinating history."

It's the story behind the story that fascinates, however. In 1975, Helmut Newton contacted the hotel to secure permission to mount a photo shoot on the premises. There was some discussion about his work, its sensual aspects, and whether this would be suitable for the Villa d'Este "image." In the end, permission was granted, as Newton was a major artist of the day who explained that it was his dream to come and do a story at Villa d'Este. The only stipulation was that the prints had to be seen in advance and approved by Villa d'Este before they appeared in the French magazine *Realites*.

Newton arrived at the hotel with his two models. He moved about the hotel taking entirely appropriate photographs of gorgeous women in fabulous locations. They were accompanied during the session by a senior hotel staff member to assist them and provide

no, george washington

alfred hitchcock

barbra
streisand

duke and duchess
of windsor

william randolph hearst

didn't sleep here, but...

caroline of monaco

mark
twain

king leopold
of belgium

...did

clark gable once
it gives you

had my room.
a heady feeling.

CLARK GABLE WITH CARLO MAGNI, VILLA D'ESTE CONCIERGE FOR 51 YEARS.

any information they needed. The photo shoot was soon completed. The *Réalites* article was sent to the hotel before publication as had been agreed, and it was beautiful. Everyone was very happy.

Some months later, the staff member who had accompanied Newton on his shoot at the hotel was in New York and invited by a friend to attend the launch of Newton's new book, *White Women*. During the

ABOVE AND OPPOSITE: HELMUT NEWTON'S FAMOUS IMAGES FROM HIS 1975 BOOK, *WHITE WOMEN*, WHICH HE PHOTOGRAPHED IN PART AT VILLA D'ESTE.

presentation, Newton mentioned that he had created a second set of photographs at Villa d'Este that did not appear in *Realites*; they were, however, included in the book. Much to the surprise of the Villa d'Este employee, he mentioned that he had managed to divert the attention of his Villa d'Este attendant and photographed more sensual, avant-garde images during the few moments when she was not present.

Fearing immediate dismissal, the Villa d'Este staff member hurried back to Como to present the "alternate" version of the photographs to her superiors. But the board members, at that time populated by elderly gentlemen, quickly seized upon the book and continued to enjoy it for years to come. Crisis averted.

The environments that have been created in each room and throughout Villa d'Este are a draw for more than the creative cognoscenti. Throughout time, visitors to the villa have come from all groups; while once favored by princes, queens, empresses, and lesser mortals, it is now the "in" place for barons of business and pop stars. And every one of them experiences the physical and spiritual comfort so well-described by Caroline of Brunswick in 1815, when she said, "I have now settled myself in a most beautiful grotto upon the Lake of Como."

VILLA D'ESTE GUEST ROOMS HAVE PRE-SERVED THE IMPRESSIVE AURA OF A NOBLE PAST. NO TWO ARE EXACTLY ALIKE IN EITHER SIZE OR DÉCOR. LEFT: A FIRST-FLOOR SUITE EXHIBITS THE PERIOD FUR-NISHINGS AND PAINTINGS AND COMO SILK FABRICS THAT DISTINGUISH DECORATION THROUGHOUT THE HOTEL.

chapter seven

risotto for two

"the place is expensive, but worth the cost because the price of the room includes the breakfast."

—JOSEPH HELLER

In 1999, when *Gourmet* magazine named Villa d'Este the third-best hotel in the world, it was largely due to the dining experiences available. With a world-renowned chef at the helm, Luciano Parolari creates both extravagant and elegant menus throughout today's Villa d'Este, mirroring the highly acclaimed meals served here from the first days that the villa began serving guests—then privately—400 years ago.

For the height of elegance and formal dining there is the Verandah restaurant, situated on the shore of Lake Como, with its spectacular glass-enclosed dining room and terrace. For casual but equally sophisticated fare there is the Grill restaurant, again offering splendid views of Lake Como. The newly installed Enoteca features the best in winetasting as its centerpiece, surrounding the wines with local and perfectly prepared small dishes. And there's always the poolside café, where even the sandwiches are created to perfection. Alexandra Mayes Birnbaum

LEFT: VILLA D'ESTE'S FAMOUS VERANDA
RESTAURANT IS SURROUNDED BY GLASS
WALLS THAT, WITH THE PUSH OF A BUT-
TON, DISAPPEAR INTO THE GROUND FOR
OPEN-AIR DINING. GLASSES ARE FOUND
UPSIDE DOWN, AS SHOWN HERE, ONLY
WHEN THE TABLES ARE SET FOR THE
DAY. THEY ARE TURNED RIGHT-SIDE UP
15 MINUTES BEFORE THE SEATING FOR
THE FIRST MEAL.

VILLA D'ESTE
Lac de Côme

Antipasto caldo
Ristretto gotta d'oro

Aragosta all'Americana

Pollanche di Romagna
Tartufi di Piemonte
Cuori di lattuga

Funghi triffolati

Soffiato
Gelato alla Certosa
Ghiottonerie

Cestini di frutta

sums it up perfectly, "For those lucky enough to have indulged in Luciano Parolari's repasts as guests at the magical Villa d'Este, these edible souvenirs evoke the fondest and tastiest memories of their stay."

Then there's the cooking school, the idea for which started 30 years ago. Twice a year, vistors come to the hotel for a weeklong cooking demonstration by Luciano Parolari. Arriving in Lake Como over a quarter century ago as a 24 year old in search of a career, Parolari today oversees a staff of 36, runs all of the restaurants, and maintains the cooking school. Like the lavish manors and meticulously manicured gardens that define Villa d'Este, Parolari creates refined, elegant, and visually stunning food.

One anecdote clearly sums up the dining experience of Villa d'Este. An elderly, regular guest of the hotel arrived at the Grill restaurant for dinner and was seated by Salvatore Piazza, the maitre d'. After perusing the menu, the woman disappointingly remarked that she would like to order the risotto—a specialty of the region—but that the dish could be ordered only for a minimum of two people. Mr. Piazza leaned toward the woman and was heard to say, "Don't worry: You order one, I'll order one!"

Not only is the food sublime, but the staff that serves it is legendary. More than 70 percent of the staff members have been with the hotel for more than 15 years. Not only do they know the dishes and menus, but they know the guests, too. With incredible efficiency that is unobtrusive but personal, this corps of experts guides each diner through a mouthwatering experience.

But not all of the extravagant Villa d'Este menus are served at Villa d'Este. The reputation of the cooking has become so widespread over the last 30 years that Parolari is often invited to pamper the palates of diners around the world, traveling to faraway locations to prepare his specialties. Thus, in 1995 he had the occasion to serve a special lunch and dinner at the United Nations' Delegates' Dining Room commemorating its 50th anniversary. Later that year, he cooked for a benefit at which the guest of honor was Kofi Annan. He has traveled to Australia and virtually all of North America to participate in charity benefits and banquets.

And then there are all those wonderful theme evenings where special meals are served to complement the event. At the imperial Austria evening, for example, the chef prepared delicacies like cabbage flan with sarnen cheese and speck from Tyrol; spaetzle in light meat sauce and perch fillets with sage; veal loin with chanterelle cream sauce, potato strudel, braised red cabbage, and Tyrolese dumplings; and finally, sacher cake with whipped cream, coffee, and, of course, the obligatory plate of cookies. These evenings, accompanied by entertainment tailored to the occasion, are memorable for all involved. But one suspects that there have been many memorable culinary events through the years at Villa d'Este.

Villa d'Este has served as a visitors' banquet hall for numerous historical events through the years, and at each an extraordinary menu was served. This began as early as 1805, when the Contessa Pino redecorated a banquet hall in the then Villa Garrovo to accommodate the visit of Napoleon and his troops for dinner—which, unfortunately, Napoleon never attended. One can only imagine the menu that would have been served to the emperor.

dining rooms

poolside
cafè

enoteca

with a view

veranda

grill
terrace

an then there's room service...

But there's no need to imagine the décor of the room, covered with imperial "N"s as it is today.

From 1834 to 1847, during the period when Austria was asserting its grip over the region, banquets were held by insurgents as a disguise for political opportunity to promote secession. One could guess that the menus then offered a slightly Austrian inclination.

More recently, Italo Balbo's air passage overseas was celebrated at Villa d'Este in 1933 with a banquet dinner in the Empire Room, which served *antipasto caldo, ristretto gotta d'oro, aragosta all' Americana, pollanche di Romagna, tartufi di Piemonte, cuori di lattuga, funghi trifolati, soffiato, gelato alla certosa, ghiottonerie,* and *cestini di frutta.* The menu also mentions that the wines were Castel Tagliolo, Chianti Stravecchio, and champagne. Because this event took place during the Fascist era, when the French and English languages were prohibited, this historic menu is printed only in Italian.

Even Evita Peron visited Villa d'Este for the day, en route to Switzerland in 1947. A banquet lunch was served, featuring *ristretto freddo all'essenza di sedani, trota salmonata del lario in bella vista, insalata di cetrioli con salsa majonese, arrosto di pollo primaverile all'Americana, fagiolini verdi al burro, patate olivette* and, for dessert, *lamponi alla Nabuel Huapi* and *frivolezze.*

In 1948, when Biki presented her autumn and winter collections at Villa d'Este, the dinner gala in the Empire Room featured *terrine de foie gras, consomme riche, paillettes d'or, truite de Ruisseau au bleu* and *pommes vapeur, aiguillettes de volaille Jeannette, salade bagatelle,* and *poires belle Helene* and *mignardises.* It is said that this meal inspired murder because later in the evening, one of the guests shot her lover at the table.

And finally, one of the "tongue-in-cheek" menus deserves mentioning, too: the celebratory dinner for Richard Condon, author of *The Abandoned Woman,* a novelization of the story of Caroline of Brunswick. Featured were smoked salmon princess of Wales, Lady Montant soup, filet of sole Brunswick, lemon sherbet Pergami, chateaubriand Villa d'Este, and strawberries queen of England.

Illustrious history aside, today's meals at Villa d'Este survive the test of time. As Chuck Williams of Williams-Sonoma reports, "For the past 15 years, whenever I want something special for lunch or dinner, I cook from one of Luciano Parolari's recipes. It is always simple but delicious and inspires a nostalgic longing for the Villa d'Este with every bite. It is the next best thing to making a trip to Lake Como."

ABOVE: MENU FROM AN EASTER LUNCH, 1931. OPPOSITE: FOR PRIVATE DINING, THE NAPOLEON ROOM PROVIDES HAUTE CUISINE AND HISTORY, TOO. IN 1805, DONNA VITTORIA INVITED NAPOLEON TO VILLA D'ESTE (THEN VILLA GARROVO). SHE SET ASIDE AN APARTMENT ON THE GROUND FLOOR FOR THE EMPEROR, DECORATING IT IN SILK AND BROCADES BEARING THE NAPOLEONIC "N." UNFORTUNATELY, NAPOLEON NEVER ARRIVED, BUT TODAY THE ROOM REMAINS IN ITS ORIGINAL STATE, AS A LOCATION FOR BANQUETS AND PRIVATE GROUP DINING. IN 1971, CHRISTIE'S HELD ITS FIRST AUCTION IN ITALY AT VILLA D'ESTE; THE NAPOLEON ROOM WAS CHOSEN FOR ITS PRIVATE BANQUETS.

chapter eight

celebrity register

"i should be happy to happy to see you in my little nutshell."

—CAROLINE OF BRUNSWICK, PRINCESS OF WALES

Villa d'Este is no stranger to notoriety. From Caroline of Brunswick to the Biki fashion-show murder, scandalous events have occurred at Villa d'Este because notorious people have been visitors. In most cases, they were notorious before they arrived—but not always. No matter how luxurious the appointments, how beautiful the location, how gorgeous the décor, how delicious the food, it is the personalities of Villa d'Este—visitors and staff alike—who have made it a continuing international sensation.

OPPOSITE: AN ELEGANT ENTOURAGE ARRIVING IN STYLE AT VILLA D'ESTE IN 1898 BY HORSE AND CARRIAGE.

ABOVE: EVITA PERON VISITED VILLA D'ESTE IN 1947. OPPOSITE, TOP: WALLIS SIMPSON AND EDWARD, PRINCE OF WALES. OPPOSITE, BOTTOM LEFT: THE FIRST PHOTOGRAPH EVER TAKEN OF THEM TOGETHER WAS SHOT AT VILLA D'ESTE AS THEY EMBARKED ON THE HOTEL LAUNCH. ONCE MARRIED, THE DUKE AND DUCHESS OF WINDSOR WERE FREQUENT VISITORS TO VILLA D'ESTE. ON EACH RETURN, THEY WOULD TAKE THE LAUNCH AT SUNSET, AT WHICH TIME WALLIS REPORTEDLY SAID, "SAME LAKE, SAME MOON, AND SAME BOAT—HOW ROMANTIC!" OPPOSITE, BOTTOM RIGHT: A PORTION OF A NOTE THAT THE DUCHESS WROTE TO THE HOTEL'S MANAGEMENT IN APPRECIATION OF HER STAY.

in these familiar
and charming surroundings.
Again with my thanks
for your charming
flight here I am
Yours sincerely
Wallis
Duchess of Windsor

It is appropriate to begin the story of the "people" of Villa d'Este with Caroline of Brunswick. Considering the times in which she lived, she was certainly a renegade. Now recognized as a highly intelligent woman, she was nonetheless very badly educated and relatively uncultured in comparison to the British royal she married. When she and her husband discovered that they were not suited for one another, she removed herself from the royal household and settled at Villa d'Este. Caroline's later affair with the Italian Bartolomeo Pergami followed by her return to England to attempt to claim her place as queen caused the king to charge her with adultery in 1820.

It is fascinating to read the press of the time and the actual court documents from her trial. They are replete with every gory detail and infraction that she supposedly committed while at Villa d'Este. But one thing we know for sure: she was the first "celebrity" to inhabit the villa in a long line to follow.

The second most notable instance of scandalous behavior involves a crime of passion at the first big social event to take place at Villa d'Este after World War II. When Mussolini declared war on France and England from the balcony of his study on Piazza Venezia in Rome on June 10, 1940, the hotel lost its international clientele and nearly went out of business. However, by 1942, when Milan was under siege, many of the richest families fled Milan and took up residence at Villa d'Este. Notwithstanding the war, this was a time when the hotel was again "swinging"—every night was a party.

By 1943, the Allied forces were pushing back the Germans from the South so that German control was limited to the North. At this point, the Germans took control of Villa d'Este, the guests were evacuated, and the hotel became a hospital where plastic surgery was performed. It was rumored that before escaping to South America, many senior Nazi officials stopped off at Villa d'Este to have their faces remade. It is possible that here many notorious Nazis became unrecognizable.

Finally, in April 1945, the Germans fled the Fifth Army; the Americans arrived in Cernobbio and Villa d'Este was liberated along with the rest of the North. According to a July 1945 *New York Times* article, Villa d'Este became the favorite rest camp for G.I.'s on leave.

By 1948, the hotel had been returned to its prewar owners and restored. A big event was scheduled for September of that year because this was the month when the "beautiful people" planned their lake vacations. Biki, the top Milanese couturier of the time, had sent out over 200 invitations for a black-tie gala dinner and fashion show to take place on September 15. The guest list included luminaries like Baron de Rothschild of Paris, who was known to never miss a good party.

At the same time that hotel manager Willy Dombré, a charming gentleman of the old school, was putting the finishing touches on the hotel for the soiree, Count Lamberto Bellentani was preparing to leave for the gala with his young wife, Pia, who was wearing an ermine cape over a sequined evening gown and some of her most precious jewels. The count commented on how beautiful she looked and said, "I think I'll get my revolver. I'll feel better if I have it on me for the return trip since you are wearing all that jewelry."

The Bellentanis were part of the new "Café Society" that had cropped up during the war years. The count had a family fortune and didn't have to work for a living; Pia, nearly 20 years his junior, was his companion

OPPOSITE: THIS NEWSPAPER CLIPPING SHOWS THE COUNTESS PIA PELLENTANI, MINUTES BEFORE SHOOTING HER LOVER AT A SOIREE IN THE NIGHTCLUB OF VILLA.D'ESTE.

hollywood on

lake como

in lavish entertainment and society. Gossipers said that theirs was a marriage of convenience. But Pia and the count were generally looked upon as a compatible couple—until their encounter with Carlo Sacchi.

Carlo Sacchi was a wealthy Como silk manufacturer with a lovely German wife and two daughters. He considered himself a godsend to women, dedicating most of his free time to the art of courting beautiful ladies and showering them with orchids and the like. He was not good-looking and his demeanor was bored and skeptical, but he seemed to attract the ladies nonetheless.

The Bellentanis and the Sacchis arrived at Villa d'Este almost simultaneously. They had reserved a table in the Empire Room, where the dinner and the fashion show were to take place. They were seated together and had previously been seen in tandem at all the major social events.

For the previous three years, it had been rumored that Pia and Carlo were in the throes of an affair. This was news, but not shockingly so; at the time, extramarital affairs were quite common and accepted in high society, as long as they were conducted with a certain discretion.

The problem was that Pia had fallen in love with Sacchi. Even knowing that he was unreliable and rather vulgar, she believed that she could "redeem" him.

Dinner went smoothly; the fashion show was on, and at two o'clock in the morning, the crowds started thinning out. The Bellentanis and the Sacchis decided to have a drink in the nightclub, and others followed suit. The scenario rapidly unfolded: A shot was fired. Carlo Sacchi was lying on his back on the dance floor, but the orchestra continued to play. At first, it appeared as though Sacchi was playing one of his practical jokes because he appeared to be grinning, even in death. Pia cried, "It's jammed! It's jammed!" as she held the loaded pistol to

CLOCKWISE FROM OPPOSITE, TOP LEFT: THE CAST OF THE SOAP OPERA *THE BOLD AND THE BEAUTIFUL* WITH GENERAL MANAGER CLAUDIO CECCHERELLI AT FAR RIGHT; FRANK SINATRA AND AVA GARDNER; BETTE DAVIS; SYLVESTER STALLONE; AND ALFRED HITCHCOCK.

her head, everyone now realizing that something ghastly had just happened.

Biki's husband began to slap Pia repeatedly; three ladies bent over Sacchi's body; the police arrived; Count Bellentani paced the hall, chainsmoking. Both Bellentanis were eventually arrested: Pia for murder, the count for carrying a handgun without a license. It turned out that Carlo Sacchi had been torturing Pia with promises of running away together, promises that

he dashed with ridicule during the party that night at Villa d'Este. The final straw came when he called her a *terrona* (peasant from the South). Insulted and hurt, Pia fired one shot at her lover through her white ermine cape. Naturally, the press had a field day with the events of the evening, clamoring, "A Convent School-Girl at Villa d'Este," "The Madame Bovary of Villa d'Este," "Drama at Villa d'Este," and, most embarrassingly, "Countess Kills Lover Who Called Her Terrona."

ABOVE: CONCIERGES ROMANO SCOTTI, NOW RETIRED AFTER 44 YEARS WITH VILLA D'ESTE, AND REMO CASTELLI, STILL GOING STRONG. OPPOSITE, TOP: THE STAFF OF THE GRILL FLANK MAITRE D' SALVATORE PIAZZA. OPPOSITE, CENTER: CAMILLO LIVI, FORMER PRESIDENT OF VILLA D'ESTE, WITH WILLY DOMBRÉ, WHOSE FAMILY RAN THE HOTEL BEGINNING IN 1896. OPPOSITE, BOTTOM: EXECUTIVE CHEF LUCIANO PAROLARI.

OPPOSITE: MARC DROULERS, FORMER PRESIDENT OF VILLA D'ESTE, AWOKE VILLA D'ESTE FROM A LONG SLEEP OF BEING NEGLECT IN THE MID-1906S. THIS PHOTO WAS TAKEN ON THE DAY HE IN-AUGURATED THE HOTEL'S FLOATING SWIMMING POOL. CLOCKWISE FROM TOP LEFT: FUTURE QUEEN AND KING OF ITALY, MARIA-JOSE OF BELGIUM AND UMBERTO DI SAVOIA, PRINCE OF PIEDMONT, VISIT VILLA D'ESTE IN 1929; FORMER ITALIAN PRESIDENT SANDRO PERTINI IN THE FOREGROUND WITH MARIO ARRIGO, FORMER MANAGER OF VILLA D'ESTE, AT RIGHT; GIANNI AGNELLI STROLLS THROUGH THE SPLENDID LOBBY WITH HOTEL MANAGER CLAUDIO CECHERELLI IN 1998; MIKHAIL AND RAISA GORBACHEV IN THE GARDEN.

For a period, business at the hotel slowed down, and it took some time before the novelty of the sensational crime wore off. In the long run, it appeared that this crime of passion actually added a veneer of glamour to the Villa d'Este image. More than 50 years later the press continues to feature the crime when talking about society and Villa d'Este. But historically, its real importance is that this was the first major postwar social event to take place in all of Italy, and it was a killer.

More recently, Villa d'Este has been pronounced "Hollywood on Lake Como" because of all the visiting film and theatrical people, including Greta Garbo, Gary Cooper, Bing Crosby, Woody Allen and Mia Farrow, Marcello Mastroianni, Mel Gibson, and Robin Williams. There is a long history of visiting luminaries, including artists—from masters such as John Singer Sargent to ex-statesman Winston Churchill, who dabbled in painting; musicians from Puccini to Madonna; fashion magnates—Bill Blass, Oscar de la Renta, and Gianfranco Ferré; literati—Walter Lippmann, Leonard Lyons, Vladimir Nabokov and John le Carré; and those on a romantic getaway—from Rita Hayworth and Orson Welles to Elizabeth Taylor and Nicky Hilton.

But there is more to the people of Villa d'Este than the visitors and guests: Today, the people who are the biggest draw to the hotel are the staff. In the words of Jean Marc Droulers, "The staff at Villa d'Este is the hotel's most treasured asset." At Villa d'Este, there is a longstanding tradition of ultracompetency combined with friendly—but never intrusive—personnel. This attitude of caring is one that is endemic and shared by both the top staff and the young boys who deliver room service. People are proud to work at Villa d'Este, proud to give the best of themselves. Droulers asserts,

"To have good staff, you need good customers because customers form the staff."

The staff is known to be discreet. Carlo Magni—a former concierge who was with the hotel for 50 years—was once featured in an article with the headline "Concierge Is Mum on Famous Guests." Magni was quoted as saying that "silence and discretion are the key words in this job." He would share only the harmless anecdotes.

Magni's prodigious memory, organizational skills, and affable personality won him friends among the powerful and famous. He was invited to Portugal in 1977 as a guest of the exiled Italian king Umberto, whom Magni first met at Villa d'Este when Umberto was still a crown prince.

Known in his circles as "the concierge of the Iron Gate" for his sharp eye, the amiable Magni remembers that more than 10,000 china ashtrays with the hotel's insignia were bought and pilfered by guests as mementos in 1979, and that Walt Disney used to ask for three hotel ashtrays each Christmas. Magni also remembers that Elizabeth Taylor still owes him three mystery books that she borrowed during her May 1950 honeymoon with Nicky Hilton at Villa d'Este. He fondly recalls the love story of the duke and duchess of Windsor and the couple's frequent visits to Villa d'Este shortly after the duke renounced the British throne in December 1936 to marry Wallis Warfield Simpson.

At Villa d'Este, it is not only the staff that has been there for generations, but many of the guests return year after year. And the wonder of it is that the newcomers feel as though they have returned to a familiar place, too, because of the atmosphere and "soul" of the surroundings. It's almost as if Villa d'Este itself were human.

OPPOSITE: EVEN JOSEPHINE BAKER COULDN'T RESIST A SNAPSHOT IN FRONT OF THE FAMED MOSAIC IN 1931.

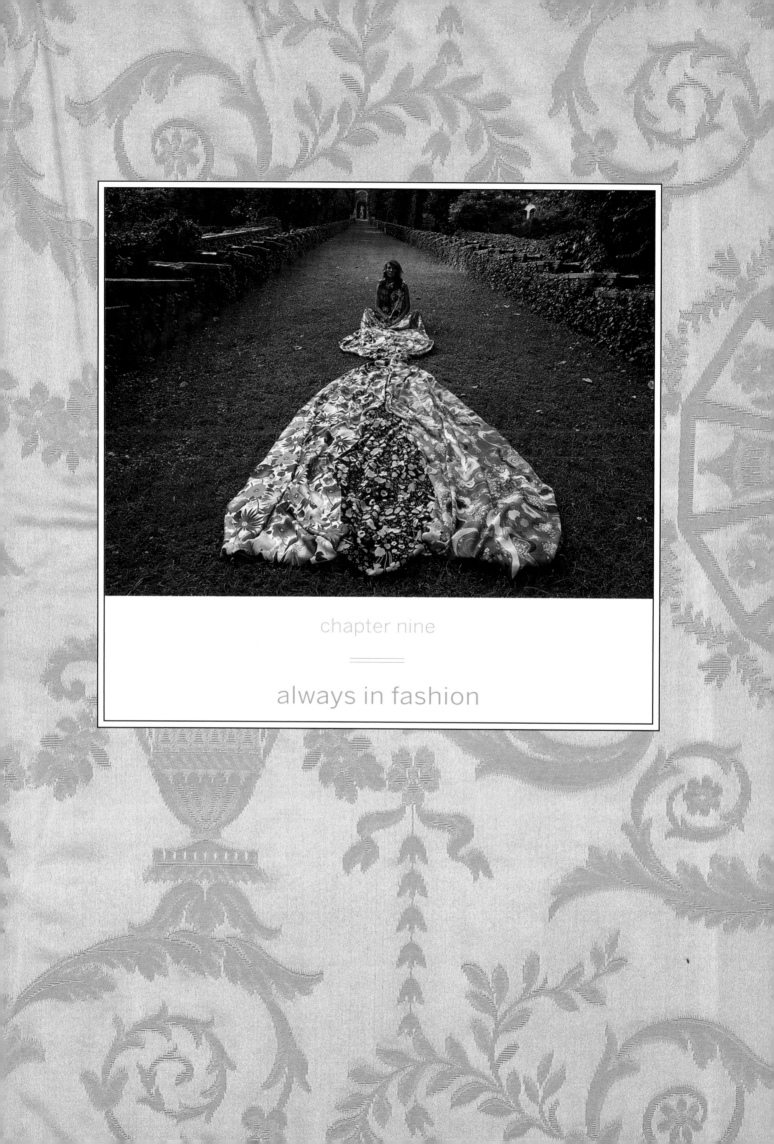

chapter nine

always in fashion

> **"for one giddy, giggly moment after seeing the hotel i'd just checked into, i wondered if i'd dare go to dinner without a tiara."**

—JANE MORSE,
SYNDICATED COLUMNIST

Lake Como is the silk capital of the world,

and from this resource has grown the international

renown of Italian designers like Missoni, Ferré, Versace, Armani, and Valentino.

The first silk looms were set up at Como in the mid-16th century, possibly as early as 1554. Development was sluggish at first, hampered by the political and fiscal difficulties of Spanish rule. Only after 1714, when the Spanish abandoned Milan, was the silk weaving trade able to enjoy a greater independence. In Como, there were

OPPOSITE: BITS OF THE FAMOUS COMO SILK HAVE BEEN COMBINED TO FORM THIS CONFECTION OF A DRESS, PHOTOGRAPHED ON THE AVENUE OF THE CYPRESSES AT VILLA D'ESTE.

FASHION AND VILLA D'ESTE HAVE BEEN LINKED FROM THE BEGINNING OF TIME. ABOVE: THE EMPIRE ROOM, LOCATED NEXT TO THE CANOVA BAR, WAS THE LOCALE FOR THIS 1930S FASHION SHOW. BELOW: LONG BEFORE THE PALAZZO PANTS OF EMILIO PUCCI BECAME THE RAGE, THE "BEAUTIFUL PEOPLE" WORE BATHING ATTIRE LIKE THAT SHOWN HERE. OPPOSITE: EVEN IN THE 1930S, THE MOSAIC INSPIRED DESIGNERS AND PHOTOGRAPHERS TO USE IT AS A BACKDROP FOR THE FASHIONS OF THE DAY.

60 looms in operation, and by 1772 there were more than 200. By the beginning of the 19th century, there were already more than 1400. A booming business was beginning to flourish.

Since World War II, Como fabric manufacturers have stolen the limelight from the French, who dominated the quality silk market in Europe for years. Italian designers have always considered themselves lucky to have their fabric sources so close at hand, and today, even top French couturiers come to Como, along with noted American and English designers.

Milan developed as a fashion center largely because it was located so close to Como. Italian fabric knowledge and expertise in working the fabric was one of the overriding factors in the success of the country's ready-to-wear designers in the 1970s, when major designers like Armani worked closely with Como manufacturers.

Fabric manufacturers like Ratti and Mantero are famous for their willingness to be innovative in design and to take financial risks as well. In fact, these firms, together with another hundred or more, found not only antique samples, but the instruments used in their manufacture. About a thousand pieces have been catalogued and are on permanent exhibition in the Villa Sucota offices in Cernobbio.

there is no doubt about it. the wonderful ambiance of villa d'este makes it the number one place to visit for a most fashionable clientele.

— BILL BLASS

Many of the textile companies in Como have been owned and operated by a single family for decades. Akin to the artist-artisan relationship of the finest Italian printers, Italian silk manufacturers treat each product as an art form, allowing for whatever extraordinary measures are needed to make it perfect.

Today, Villa d'Este functions as a hot spot for fashion in terms of both the important designers who retreat here and the guests who come to the region for its extraordinary fashion, using Villa d'Este as a showcase to wear it. Although the dress code at the hotel is fairly loose today, most of the visitors welcome the opportunity to dress in high style; it is rare to see a badly outfitted guest.

Lorenzo Riva, formerly Balenciaga's art director and one of the top stars of the region, is frequently seen at Villa d'Este. His fashion is created not just for the runway, but to be worn. His innate understanding of the female form and how it looks best is a trademark of his designs. "In my opinion, the creator ought to allow the woman to take a minimum initiative, otherwise the gentlewoman doesn't feel the need to build up her own charm," says Lorenzo, a master of style.

Beppe Spadacini is one of the up-and-coming fashion designers of the region. He can be seen not only relaxing at Villa d'Este, but concocting glamorous fashion shows for special "theme" evenings. His

OPPOSITE: THE FAMOUS FLOATING POOL.

designs are less haute couture and more accessible than some of the other designers and show his affinity for the tropical. His colors and shapes are free, and his unique garments are hand-painted, using fabrics like organdy and net.

As a center where the tasteful gather today as they have for centuries, Villa d'Este delivers its fashion in the same mode as it delivers its amenities, or, in the words of Jane Morse, the way Laurence Olivier delivers Shakespeare: It's all sublimely normal.

CLOCKWISE FROM TOP LEFT: A WEDDING GOWN BY DESIGNER LORENZO RIVA, WHO VISITS VILLA
D'ESTE NEARLY EVERY WEEKEND FOR INSPIRATION; RIVA WITH FREQUENT HOTEL GUEST DINA
FERRARI (LEFT), WHO WEAR ONE OF HIS DESIGNS; BEPPE SPADACINI DESIGNED THESE SILK
SCARVES; SPADACINI IS A NATIVE SON WHO HAS GATHERED INCREASD FAME IN THE FASHION
WORLD. OPPOSITE: THIS 1924 ILLUSTRATION DEPICTS VINTAGE FASHIONS ON THE TERRACE OF
VILLA D'ESTE.

LAC DE COME

MANTEAUX DE FOURRURE, DE MAX-A. LEROY

IT IS SAID THAT WHEN THE SEAGULL SITS ON THE PILINGS AND SCREECHES, THE SEASON IS OVER

The first time I went to Villa d'Este at
Lake Como I wrote something like,
"The exact location of heaven is not
known, but it may very well be here,"
and I see no reason to change that.

—HERB CAEN, SEPTEMBER 1993

"CONCORSO D'ELEGANZA VILLA D'ESTE" FOR VINTAGE CARS - SINCE 1929.

index

NOTE: PAGE NUMBERS IN ITALICS REFER TO ILLUSTRATIONS.

photo credits

ALL PHOTOGRAPHS ARE COURTESY OF VILLA D'ESTE EXCEPT THE FOLLOWING:

VILLA
D'ESTE

LAC DE COMO

CERNOBBIO

historical

highlights

1821
Prince Torlonia, the Roman banker in possession of the deed of sale of Villa d'Este, inherits the villa after Caroline's death since she never returned the bank loans.

1873
A group of Milanese businessmen form a company, purchase Villa d'Este, and open it as a luxury hotel.

1856
Baron Ciani builds the trompe l'oeil Queen's Pavilion in honor of Caroline of Brunswick, queen of England, and opens it up to the public as a spa.

1939
Joachim von Ribbentrop, the German foreign minister, and Galeazzo Ciano, the Italian foreign minister, sign the Iron Pact at Villa d'Este.

1829-1834
Prince Domenico Orsini becomes the owner of Villa d'Este.

| 1820 | 1821 | 1829 | 1834 | 1856 | 1868 | 1870 | 1873 | 1926 | 1939 |

1821-1829
The villa falls into a period of abandonment. Hordes of tourists and souvenir hunters descend upon Lake Como to view the famous villa and its gardens.

1868-1870
Villa d'Este is leased to the czarina of Russia, Maria Federowna.

1926
Villa d'Este's golf club opens at Montorfano.

and luso, with e Count

l. To she r him e

1834-1868
Baron Ciani purchases the villa and revives it.

1568
The cardinal of Como, Tolomeo Gallio, builds a villa on the site and names it Villa Garrovo after the stream that flows into the lake.

1784
The aging Milanese playboy Marquis Bartolomeo Calderara inherits the villa.

1607-1782
After the cardinal dies, the House of Gallio reigns uncontested on the shores of Cernobbio for nearly two centuries.

49 B.C.
Julius Caesar sends 5,000 Roman citizens including 500 Greek slaves to colonize Como, then known as *Novum Comum.*

1815-182
Caroline of Brunswick princess of Wales an future queen England, makes he royal entry. She change the name to Villa d'Est

49 B.C.	1442	1568	1607	1615	1782	1784	1806	1815

1782-1784
Carlo Tolomeo, the last of the Gallios, sells the property to Count Ruggero Marliani.

1442
Cernobbio, located three miles from the town of Como, remains an obscure hamlet populated only by fishermen and woodcutters until the 15th century.

A handful of nuns takes refuge in a small convent known as the Cloister of Sant' Andrea (today the location of Villa d'Este's park). Ruins on the site are believed to have belonged to the nunnery.

1615
The Sultan of Morocco arrives with his retinue to see the reported splendors of the cardinal's villa for himself.

1806
The marquis dies, his wife, Vittoria P a former ballerina La Scala, inherits t villa. She marries Domenico Pino, a young, handsome Napoleonic genera keep him amused, builds fortresses fo so that he can stag mock war battles.

i d'Este du côté du lac de Come.

40   50   60   70   80   de Milan

AN ETCHING OF VILLA D'ESTE IN 1825

1976
Executive chef
Luciano Parolari cooks
at his first of many
charity dinners in the
United States.

1997
All 166 guest rooms
are renovated and
decorated by Roberta
Droulers. No
two rooms are alike
in size or décor.

1999
A spa opens in the
Cardinal's Building,
featuring personal
indulgences such as
massage and facials.

Villa La Massa wel-
comes its first guests.

tel cele-
ts centen-
th year-
festivities.

or pool
d to the
y.

1986
An underground
garage is built.

| 1975 | 1976 | 1977 | 1986 | 1995 | 1997 | 1998 | 1999 | 2000 |

1997
The Mosaic Wing
opens with 12
new rooms.

In November,
Luciano Parolari
travels to the
United States to
prepare a
gala dinner at
the United
Nations in honor
of Kofi Annan.

2000
An underground
passage connects
the spa to the
Sporting Club.

1975
The disco opens.

1977
Villa d'Este's cooking
school goes on the
road: Demonstrations
of the hotel's cuisine
are given on tours
throughout the United
States and Australia.

1998
Luciano Parolari
goes to Dallas,
Texas: in November
to cook at a dinner
to benefit the
Parkinson's Disease
Association.

The hotel
purchases a
property in
Florence,
Villa La Massa.

1944
Villa d'Este serves as a
German hospital at the tail
end of World War II.

1971
Christie's of
London holds its
first auction in
Italy in the
Empire Room.

1973
The h•
brates
nial w
round

An inc
is add•
prope:

1947
The hotel reopens.

1966
Many enhancements
are made to the
hotel: The floating
swimming pool is
installed, the
Sporting Club opens,
and a new restaurant,
the Grill, is added.

1942	1944	1945	1947	1948	1966	1969	1971	1972	1973

1942
Wealthy Milanese
live at Villa d'Este
during the Milan
bombing.

1969
The nightclub
opens.

1948
In the early-morning
hours of September 16,
Pia Bellentani shoots
her lover, Carlo Sacchi,
at the Biki fashion show,
the first major postwar
event at Villa d'Este.

1945
On April 25,
Mussolini and his
mistress, Claretta
Petacci, are captured
in the nearby town
of Dongo and shot
in Mezzegra.

Villa d'Este is used
as a rest camp for
the United States
Fifth Army. Five
hundred soldiers are
sent with orders "to
enjoy themselves."

1972
Cooking classes begin